D0197112

Bear Grylls was brought up on the Isle of father taught him to climb and sail. A martial arts expert, Bear went on to spend three years as a soldier in the British Special Forces (21 SAS). He then had a free-fall parachuting accident in Africa, breaking his back in three places. Despite this, and after months of military rehabilitation, he went on to become one of the youngest ever climbers to reach the summit of Mount Everest.

Bear is the host of Discovery Channel's Emmy-nominated TV series *Man Vs Wild* (also known as *Born Survivor*) which is one of the most watched shows on the planet, reaching an estimated 1.2 billion viewers. Bear continues to lead record-breaking expeditions, from Antarctica to the Arctic, which in turn have raised over $2.5 million for children around the world.

Bear was appointed as the youngest ever Chief Scout on record, as figurehead to 28 million Scouts worldwide. He was made a Lieutenant-Commander in the Royal Navy, and is a best-selling author. He now lives with his wife, Shara, and their three sons, Jesse, Marmaduke and Huckleberry, on a Dutch barge in London and on a small remote Welsh island.

'I cannot think of anybody I know who has faced the challenges and overcome them like Bear Grylls . . . I greatly admire him'

GENERAL THE LORD GUTHRIE OF CRAIGIEBANK,
GCB LVO OBE, COLONEL COMMANDANT OF THE SAS

'A truly magnificent achievement, and one that set alight the imagination of so many in this country . . . it's been a privilege for the Royal Navy to have been involved in such an historic event'

ADMIRAL SIR ALAN WEST,
KCB DSC ADC, FIRST SEA LORD

Also by Bear Grylls

FACING UP

BEAR GRYLLS

FACING THE FROZEN OCEAN

ONE MAN'S DREAM TO LEAD A TEAM
ACROSS THE TREACHEROUS
NORTH ATLANTIC

PAN BOOKS

First published 2004 by Macmillan

This edition published 2011 by Pan Books
an imprint of Pan Macmillan, a division of Macmillan Publishers Limited
Pan Macmillan, 20 New Wharf Road, London N1 9RR
Basingstoke and Oxford
Associated companies throughout the world
www.panmacmillan.com

ISBN 978-0-330-42707-4

9

A CIP catalogue record for this book is available from
the British Library.

Typeset by SetSystems Ltd, Saffron Walden, Essex
Printed and bound by CPI Group (UK) Ltd, Croydon, CR0 4YY

To my dad, who I miss so much,

and to Shara for giving me Jesse, our little son,

whom my father would so adore.

mer′cy *n. & a.*
1. compassion towards those in distress;
2. something for which to be thankful;
3. a blessing – 'it was a mercy we got out alive'

Dear Bear,

    I was mightily relieved to hear that you had returned safely from your terrifying ordeal! I think I remember warning you that the North Atlantic was not exactly the nicest place to be in an open boat, but you clearly experienced some truly awful conditions and I am full of admiration for the way that you and your team coped. I am thankful that my message to you arrived just in time – but I cannot possibly imagine it was at all adequate to sustain you during those freezing and frightening conditions..!

    The photographs tell your tale very well and I imagine that your talks are sell-outs, which is, of course, excellent news for The Prince's Trust! It really is so good of you to allow my Trust to benefit from all these endeavours and I can assure you that the money you raise will make an enormous difference to many lives.

    This comes, as ever, with my boundless admiration for you and your intrepid colleagues and my heartfelt thanks for all you have done for my Trust.

Yours most sincerely,

Charles

CONTENTS

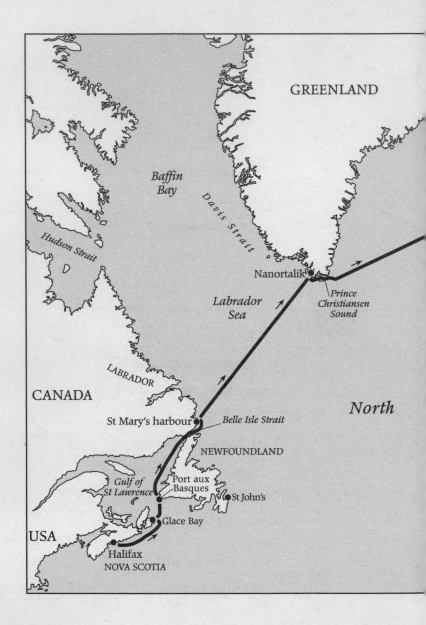

GREENLAND

Baffin
Bay

Davis Strait

Hudson Strait

Nanortalik

*Prince
Christiansen
Sound*

*Labrador
Sea*

LABRADOR

CANADA

North

St Mary's harbour

Belle Isle Strait

NEWFOUNDLAND

*Gulf of
St Lawrence*

Port aux
Basques

St John's

Glace Bay

USA

Halifax
NOVA SCOTIA

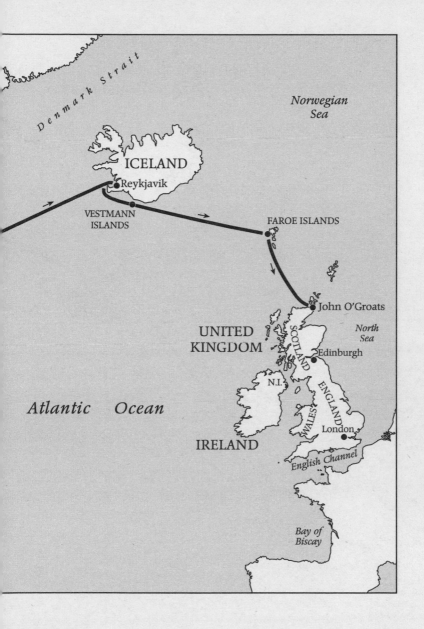

1. DANGEROUS DREAMS

The man who risks nothing, gains nothing.

Neil Armstrong

We are still no closer to Base-Camp and it's getting late. I glance nervously around the Icefall. We are 19,000 vertical feet above sea level, in the mouth of Everest's killer jaws. I notice my hand is shaking as I fumble with the ropes through thick mittens. I am scared.

The sound of the metal climbing devices clinking on my harness is becoming hypnotic. I squeeze my eyes tight shut then open them. I try to breath rhythmically. I dig my crampons into the snow and wait. Mick is still ten yards away, stepping carefully across the broken blocks of ice. We have been in this crevasse-ridden, frozen death-trap for over nine hours and we are tiring. Fast.

I stand up on my feet and take a few more careful steps, testing the ice with each movement. Then I feel the ice crack under me. I hold my breath. My world stands still. It cracks again then drops and opens up beneath me. I am falling.

As I smash against the grey wall of the crevasse that was hidden beneath a thin veneer of ice, my world is spinning. The tips of my crampons catch the edge of the crevasse wall and the force throws me to the other side, crushing my shoulder and arm against the ice. I carry on falling, then suddenly I jerk to a halt as the rope somehow holds me. I can hear my screams echoing in the darkness below.

The ice that is still falling around me crashes against my skull, jerking my head backwards. I lose consciousness for a few precious seconds. I come to, and watch the ice falling away beneath me into the darkness as my body gently swings around on the end of the rope. Suddenly all is eerily silent.

Adrenalin is soaring around my body, and I find myself shaking in waves of convulsions. I scream again and the sound echoes around the walls. I look up to the ray of light above, then down to the abyss below. Panic is overwhelming me. I clutch frantically for the wall, but it is glassy smooth. I swing my ice-axe at it wildly, but it doesn't hold, and my crampons screech across the ice. In desperation I clutch the rope above me and look up.

I am 23 years of age and about to die.

The River Thames, September 2003, five years later. It is raining. I look up and hope for better weather for the day of Jesse's christening. I have it all planned.

The priest is going to stand on the old wooden deck of our barge, his robes billowing in the autumn breeze that whistles down the Thames, and, right there, with our families all around, he will christen our gorgeous son, Jesse, with snow water brought back from the summit of Mount Everest.

But first there were forms to be completed and my wife, Shara, was gradually working through the questions.

'Occupation?'

'What?'

'I have to put your occupation here.'

'OK.'

'Well,' Shara asked, 'what *is* your occupation?'

I hated this question. What would have been a simple query for most people was anything but straightforward for me.

It would be so much easier just to be an estate agent. It would be so simple to write.

Explorer? Sounds self-important.

Mountaineer? Well I have always climbed, I guess.

Motivational speaker? Partly, but that's not all.

Television presenter? When bribed.

Writer? Once in a while, but not that brilliant.

'Just put anything,' I replied unhelpfully.

In truth I feel rather as though I'm unemployable; but somehow I seem to have carved out this strange existence where I am able to do what feels natural to me, and then earn my living speaking about those experiences. And that, I guess, is my job.

'Oh, just put estate agent, my love,' I told her.

The two adjectives most often attached to the men and women who live these adventures are 'brave' and 'eccentric', but to be honest, I dislike them both. I am not especially brave: I struggle with so many things and am much too sensitive for my own good. I often feel both afraid and vulnerable in this weird world we live in, and miss my family if I leave them for twenty-four hours. As for 'eccentric', I am not eccentric: yes, I sometimes take risks, but by nature I am extremely cautious. I am only too aware of the law of averages: the more times you get lucky, the worse your odds become.

What I do know is that I have always tried to live as my dad taught me.

My father died less than three years ago. Out of the blue, unannounced. He had been recovering from a pacemaker operation and was at home and fine, sitting up in bed. A minute later he was dead – just like that. That wasn't meant to happen; he was only sixty-six. In the blink of an eye, one cold February morning, my dad had gone. All I had now was what he had taught me. I wish every day I could remember more.

Throughout my childhood in and around the Isle of Wight, he'd taught me to climb and he'd taught me to sail. I adored every day we spent together on the cliffs, every day on the sea. I adored the excitement, the thrill and the challenge, but above all I loved just being close to him.

I remember those special days all the time, often at odd moments. Maybe backstage at a big conference when I'm nervous, about to go out there and face another sea of strange faces. It can feel like the loneliest place on earth. I often think of Dad in those seconds before going onstage. I don't know why.

I remember how he once gave me an old 7-foot wooden boat with an even older 1-hp outboard engine. For Christmas he added a steering wheel, so I could potter around the harbour like a real captain.

He guided me, he moulded me and he liberated me.

'Now listen, Bear,' he would say. 'There are only two things that really matter in life. The first is to have dreams. The second is to look after your friends. The rest is detail.' That was life in a nutshell.

If my school reports were terrible, as they invariably were, he would say I should try harder, but it never seemed like the end of the world. He would pull a silly face, speak in a silly voice and hold me tight. And I learned more about life in those moments than in all my years of school.

It was soon after my eighth birthday that Dad gave me a huge framed photo of Mount Everest. This was immediately hung on the wall in my bedroom. I would stare at it for hours in the dark, trying to imagine what it would be like to climb up there. What would it really feel like, so far away, so exposed, in those storm-force conditions that inhabit high ice faces? In my little bedroom, that Everest dream was born. One day, I swore to myself, I would stand on top of the world.

After leaving school, I joined the army. During this time I served for three years as a soldier with the British Special Air Service (21 SAS) until a freak parachuting accident almost ended my life.

I was in southern Africa, it was early evening, everything was routine; then my chute failed to deploy properly. I survived the fall, the torn canopy slowing my descent, but my injuries were bad. I had broken my back in three places and was deemed by the African doctor a 'miracle man' to have survived. It had indeed been a miracle, and one I thank God for every day.

Six months in and out of military rehabilitation healed the bones but my confidence took much longer to return. The idea of climbing Everest seemed nothing but a pipe-dream now.

But from where I lay, I began to dream again. And as my movement increased I began to get restless. I soon found that my hunger to climb had returned, and that hunger became the focus of my recovery. When, two years later, the opportunity to join a team of three other climbers on Everest came around, every ounce of me knew this was my break. It was crazy, but here was my chance.

I had been earning about £45 a day as a soldier and I needed £15,000 for the expedition. I sold all I could, took out loans and got lucky with one amazing sponsor, Davis Langdon and Everest. The door had creaked open.

Together with Mick Crosthwaite, my friend since we were kids in the Isle of Wight, and an exceptional team led by Neil Laughton, an old army friend, I spent three extraordinary months on Everest. Finally, at 7.22 a.m. on 26 May 1998, exhausted as dawn broke over the high Himalayas, two of us from our team stood on the roof of the world. A strange combination of luck, friendship and heart had enabled that moment to come true for me. It was all that I had imagined it would be and more.

Two years later, I led a team that managed to circumnavigate Britain on jet-skis in aid of the RNLI. It was Shara's and my first summer of married life together, and not quite her ideal holiday, driving around behind us in a camper van laden with jerry cans. She thought it was crazy but we had a blast. We had the proper sponsorship, we were helping a charity, we were with my closest mates and we were following a dream. This became my career.

I had been drawn into the world of expeditions partly because it was what I loved but largely because I found it was one of the few things I could do all right.

Early in 2000, I read about a British team that had previously attempted to cross the North Atlantic, just below the Arctic Circle, in an open rigid inflatable boat (RIB). They had performed heroically in horrendous conditions. Close to hypothermia and fighting frostbite, they had twice had to put out a call for emergency help – once to be brought out of the pack ice near Greenland and on the other occasion to be lifted on to a fishing trawler during a storm off Iceland. But they completed their route and had all returned alive.

I was intrigued.

'Do you think it is possible to complete this North Atlantic crossing in an open RIB without needing such emergency assistance?' I began to ask various maritime friends.

Typically, they would laugh. I would look at them and wait, expecting an answer which never came.

'It must be,' I would then tell myself. 'It has to be possible to do.'

The idea lingered.

There had been a Hollywood film set in the same seas, *The Perfect Storm*, starring George Clooney, about a group of fishermen who set out and never came back. I had seen it already and been terrified. I watched it again, but this time differently. I scrutinized the scenario and the conditions – the way the waves and the storm formed. I tried to imagine how a small open boat would cope. What decisions would I take as skipper? Would I turn round or risk the vessel? Suddenly, almost without knowing it, I was hooked.

Icebergs, gale-force winds, whales, the Labrador Sea ... I started to sleep badly at night, my mind a race of imaginings. But most importantly, by day, solid research led me to believe the crossing was distinctly possible.

Three years later, we did it – just. This is the story of that journey across the freezing, ice-ridden, most northerly part of the Atlantic.

In late 2002, I was invited to write an introduction for *Debrett's People of Today*. I felt unsure about what to say. I wanted to explain the essence of exploration and why it still appeals so much to me. But that essence is extremely hard to capture. This was my best effort:

> *Exploration, I have discovered, is all about taking that one extra step. When you're nearing the pinnacle of a high-altitude mountain, breathing wildly, with your physical reserves run dry, and are reduced to crawling on your knees, it is heart that matters. It is heart that tips the balance between dragging yourself one step nearer to the summit,*

and turning back for the safety of camp. And it is in these critical moments and decisions that people distinguish themselves.

I don't think any of our team felt particularly distinguished or individually brilliant, me included; we were a group of well-trained and hungry young guys, but we had a bond, something special that held us together when it was bleak and cold and frightening. That bond is hard to define, but it's because of that bond that I explore. It is why I went in the first place, and it is because of that bond that we all came home.

And it is this 'coming home' that, in the world of exploration, is all that ever really matters.

2. BUILDING THE BEST

If you want to build a ship, before you give men tools, teach them to yearn for the vast and endless sea.

Antoine de Saint-Exupéry

The one niggle that I always had was how would I tell one of my crew's family if something went truly wrong out there? In the middle of the night, 400 miles from any landmass, in driving rain and sleet, you are so vulnerable.

Trying to move around a small, open boat with inflatable tubes that are slippery as hell and freezing is a lottery. But even in the worst conditions things needed to be done. You couldn't really avoid having to move around the boat. One slip, a careless move, and in giant waves in pitch darkness, at 25 knots, recovery of a man overboard would be near impossible, however hard we tried.

How would I tell his family? What words would justify my pursuit of this dream? No dream is worth a man's life. And I knew the buck would always stop with me. It kept me awake often.

This expedition was always going to be different. In the past, certainly on Everest, I had been happy to sit in the back row at meetings, to listen to the leader of the expedition and do as he asked. It was also my prerogative, every now and then, to have a grumble like everyone else. I was OK at being one of the crew, a follower. I quite liked it.

Now, suddenly, it was going to be me making those

difficult calls, taking the lead. It was a big deal for me and it made me very nervous. I was heading into an infamously dangerous part of the world, and men's lives would hang on my decisions. Not just any men's lives, but my friends' lives.

I did not particularly seek leadership – it just happened. Leadership is a hard thing to learn, but our past experiences have much to tell us. We've all known people who have shaped our lives – schoolteachers, instructors – but what makes some of them remembered with affection and others so feared? For me, the people who had shown me real leadership – in fact, more than that, people I would have been prepared to fight alongside and die with, especially from my military days – were the ones who made me feel special, who went out on a limb for me: my patrol sergeant who shared his last capful of water with me after four days in the desert; the man who said I was OK and stood up for me when it counted.

Neil Laughton had been an incredible leader on the Everest expedition, a friend and a man I could depend on, decisive at times when others might easily have hesitated. I thought of him and tried to think how I like to be led. I guessed that was a good place to start. It was simple: I always felt best when I was trusted, when I felt that what I did mattered, when I was responsible for an area of expertise. When the rope, or the oxygen, or the food, or whatever it was, was up to me.

So I wanted each of my team to assume responsibility in his own area and take a real stake in this expedition. I wanted him to make decisions and feel pride in what he was doing. I didn't want to be one of those leaders who tries to do everything, inevitably makes mistakes and ends up being resented by everyone. I didn't want it to be about me; I wanted it to be about us, together, doing our best.

When word went out among the maritime community about this project, CVs started to pour in – ten years of experience here, fifteen there, everyone was an expert, and everyone seemed to want a piece of the action. But for me they missed what I felt really counted in a team. I wanted people who weren't 'experts', I wanted people, yes, who were well trained and competent, but above that I wanted people to whom this expedition really mattered. People who would put their everything into it, their heart and soul, their enthusiasm, their reputation if it all went wrong; people who would be there in the bad times as well as the good.

I wanted people I knew and trusted, people who, when they hadn't slept for days and their hands were so cold and wet that they were wrinkled, blue and shaking, would still summon up from somewhere inside the ability to get on their hands and knees at 3 a.m. during a storm and rummage to find you an energy bar from the sodden food sack. That was the sort of person I wanted.

I was looking for people who were kind before they were brave, honest before they were brilliant. People who occasionally needed reassurance but who, when the chips were down, I felt would find something deep inside them that is special. It's called heart. I wasn't interested in people who were never scared – courage is not the absence of fear, but rather the understanding that fear is human and that we all have the ability to overcome it. I was looking for people who wanted the chance to find that something inside – that part that often surprises us, a part that is gut and instinct, and that is better than we often expect.

This is a something that people rarely get the chance to find.

If I was going to take an open, rigid inflatable boat into those inhospitable waters, I was going to make sure that I had people on whom I could rely. In the end, I picked friends.

The first name on the team was Mick Crosthwaite, first and foremost, if I'm honest, because he was my buddy. We had known each other for as long as either of us could remember, from childhood days, all the way through school, the army and then as climbing partners on the Everest expedition.

Over the years Mick has grown to represent a source of solid friendship, sound judgement and real support. His presence always seems so strong; somehow, with him, I never have to look over my shoulder to check, never have to cast a precautionary glance. I just know I can rely on him 100 per cent of the time. And that's very rare.

By nature Mick is incredibly single-minded. When he's at work, running the Tiscali network, the pan-European network-marketing arm of the Internet communications company, nothing else gets in his way. Likewise when he is on an expedition, he moves into a different zone and focuses totally on that.

Sure enough, on the day when he was due to fly from London to Canada for the start of our voyage, Mick arrived at Heathrow airport in his business suit, having rushed from some high-powered meeting where he had clinched, to quote him, 'a massive deal'. To the amazement of several bystanders, he then proceeded to change into his expedition gear right there in the drop-off zone at Terminal Four. His mobile was switched off and stayed off until he was back in Scotland, a 6,000-mile round trip away.

Mick's demanding work commitments meant he was unable to make as much of a contribution to the planning stages as he knew he should, and on several occasions this irritated me. At one point I told him that if he wanted to be part of this, that had to start now: 'I am not another of your employees to be curt with, Mick, get out of work mode and realize you need to start giving a little too much rather than a little too little to this expedition. Everyone is busting a gut and all they see is you leaving early or arriving late. It's not acceptable and you know it.' The phone went silent, not dead, just silent. He was thinking. 'Make a choice, Miguel.'

This was an important and difficult conversation, but it changed everything in the run-up. The others needed to know Mick would start putting his heart into what we were doing now, not just on the actual expedition itself. This was different from climbing. The logistics here were more complex than for a small team on a mountain and we needed everyone's energy in the preparation as much as when we would leave. What Mick didn't do, someone else had to – and it was too early on for people to feel resentment. It was all the more poignant because the others were now working so hard towards the expedition.

'I've got to go now, Mick.' And I replaced the receiver.

Mick arrived at the next meeting with the biggest file of meteorological data you've ever seen. As our weatherman, he was now in. He'd been the first to join me on the team but really the last to become one of us. But that didn't matter; what was important was that I had my wingman again.

I suppose our friendship was genuinely forged on Everest. We climbed together throughout, but in the final moments of those three months, when fate and weather and health proved decisive in selecting who finally stood on the roof of the world and who didn't, fate chose me. I was luckier, that was all.

Mick had climbed to within 350 feet of the summit when he ran out of oxygen. Soon he was slumped in the snow at 28,500 feet, dying. I had spoken to him on the radio from down at Camp Two. He calmly told me he reckoned he had ten minutes to live. Then he went quiet on the radio and wouldn't respond. I was over 5,000 feet below him, powerless to help as my best friend's life slowly ebbed away. And in my panic all I could think of was how I was ever going to tell his family.

During this time Neil Laughton found him, helped him to stand up, and together they stumbled down the ridge under the south summit. Exhaustion was too much for Mick though and two hours later, delirious, he slipped and fell almost 500 feet. In truth he should have died, but he survived, was rescued and eventually came back down from the mountain. He knew exactly how close he had been to death.

His response to our time on Everest, particularly after I finally reached the summit, underpins my admiration for him. I think it is a credit to him that he has never felt the need to go back to Everest and try again. He just feels lucky to be alive. To risk everything again to try to climb that extra 350 feet is not a risk worth taking. As so many climbers have learned the hard way, our team included, if you play the odds of one in eight climbers not returning alive from Everest's summit too often, you don't always win.

Some people say the summit of a mountain is everything. They're wrong. Staying alive is everything. The press had no interest in the fact that Mick climbed higher than K2. To them he 'failed' to reach the top. But to me, we reached the top together, there was no difference.

I once read that a true friend revels in your success when things are going well and is there for you in difficult times. Well, Mick has been exactly that kind of friend for me. And that's why it mattered so much that he should be with me this time.

The next challenge for both of us was to tell his parents. I thought he should do this himself.

'Mick, you're grown up, for God's sake, don't be a wet blanket,' I told him, eager that it should be he who announced the news and faced his mother's disquiet, not me. 'And don't just procrastinate and let them find out through a newspaper. You're unbelievable. You're like an ostrich, burying your head in the sand. Well, I tell you, I'm not getting the blame for this one while you walk quietly by smirking.'

Our families had been extremely close and had known each other for as long as I could remember. Mick's father was my grandfather's godson and both our mums are called Sally. However, despite all this, I was always a little bit nervous around his mum near expedition times. This had all started when, aged sixteen, Mick and I had announced that we were saving up to do a parachute jump together and we were off the next day. For some reason, this wasn't Mick's fault but mine. In the Crosthwaite household it had somehow become accepted wisdom that it was always unreliable Bear who got honest Mick into dangerous situations. They bought into it every time.

The parachute jump, unsuitable girls, the army, Everest – to this day, somehow, it is all my fault.

Nigel Thompson lives not much more than 100 yards away from our barge on the Thames in London. He knew Shara first, and shared a house with her while we were going out. But since then he has become a close of friend of mine as well. We eat far too many Danish pastries together in our local square, laugh lots and talk about Hussein and Mohammed, the local curry-house waiters, on a daily basis. He has the wickedest sense of humour of anyone I know, and a vulnerability that is gorgeous.

What is it that makes some people get along? Well, we laugh at the same things, we laugh easily. I think that's important. But there's more to it than that. We're comfortable together, and that's a good thing in a friend. Nige is also godfather to our little son, Jesse.

He has always had a passion for sailing and boats, and was a fanatical rower at both school and university. Despite my being a bit suspicious of his worryingly high level of interest in navigational gadgets, his favourite pastime was getting into trouble in little boats – and naturally, as so often happens with the sea, this made us the best of boating buddies.

I have been to more boat shows with Nige than with anyone else, and have talked more with him about RIBs than is healthy. I knew he had never tasted the extreme environments that the expedition would encounter to such a degree before but he had this latent hunger to do more with his life, to be a bit different. His knowledge, his energy, his enthusiasm to be part of this adventure would, I knew, make Nige the most lovely of people to share the dream with.

I will never forget one particular day at the London Boat Show with Nige. We had been wandering around, chatting to as many different RIB builders and designers as possible. I was beginning to flag, but not Nige. He was in full swing.

'But can the sheer bow still allow sufficient water clearance in a following sea?' he would ask. And they would be off. Talking terms I could hardly understand. I needed some air.

'Nige, let's come back here later maybe?' I suggested.

He reluctantly agreed; the boat-builder reached out to shake his hand and passed him his business card.

'If I can ever help in any way, any advice, whatever it is, just let me know. If you are really going to do this expedition, you need the best RIB ever built. Just give me a call.'

Nige thanked him. There was a pause as the designer waited for his response. Nige fumbled. Finally, he reached into his pocket, pulled out one of his property surveyor business cards and handed that over.

'Likewise,' he said, 'if I can ever offer *you* any help with ...' He paused '... with buying a shopping centre. Just let me know,' he finished buoyantly. The man stood bewildered as we walked away. Shopping centre? What the hell was he on about?

Nige's sense of humour never faltered. In the cold times ahead, when he began to suffer frostbite in his feet as we emerged from the Icelandic storm, he still managed to mumble to me over the wind, 'How do you think Mohammed the curry waiter would cope with this right now, right here, balancing forty poppadoms on his trolley?'

I asked Nige right at the start if he would join the expedition, and he didn't hesitate. He was working for Lunson Mitchenall, a firm of London surveyors. But this was his chance to do something more, something extraordinary, and he knew it. Most important, he went for it, and that's not always easy to do.

For me, one of the most rewarding aspects of these adventures is that they can become a genuinely life-changing experience. I've seen it so often. It gives people pride. It may be very quiet but it's there. And it's a great thing to see.

Right from the start, Nige proved a huge support to me. We discussed the expedition endlessly, and he helped me prepare the brochures that we sent out to prospective sponsors. He would stay up late at home on weeknights to print out another batch for me. They'd always be dropped off at the barge by morning. I know that I would never have got the expedition off the ground without him.

It was with Nige that I'd spend hours gathering information, constantly weighing up the pros and cons of routes, boat designs, equipment and every aspect of the expedition. Some of what we were doing as a team was new to him, and he was one of two team members who had not had the benefit of a military training, but as time went on he responded and picked things up remarkably quickly.

My nature is to speak my mind – I always have. I dislike petty jibes or undertones, I would prefer someone to say what they mean up front. It comes from having an older sister. I think it's best to try to be honest and clear the air, even if it makes us very vulnerable. What matters is that I know everyone in the long term appreciates honesty.

One evening I felt Nige was being difficult about something and I just came out with it. 'What's up, Nige? Why did you say that?' He mumbled something and we carried on, and to be honest I forgot all about it. Until three o'clock the following morning, that is, when Nige rang to say he couldn't sleep because he'd been worrying about what he'd said. He was sorry and hadn't meant it. I told him it was fine, it was nothing – it wasn't. I was impressed though. That sort of thing is not always easy to do. But Nige is that kind of sensitive, endearing person. He makes the calls we all so often put off. I knew he would be an important man to have on board.

Charlie Laing was a year ahead of me at school. We'd always known each other and got along pretty well, but we'd never been close friends. I probably only saw him twice during the ten years that had passed since we had left, maybe across the room at a party.

Then he telephoned me out of the blue. Shara and I were living in Chamonix, in the Alps, at the time, and Charlie had gone to considerable lengths to get our telephone number. He asked if he could meet me to talk about this next expedition and said he would email over his CV. Since school he had become a freelance cameraman, and had put together an impressive portfolio: among other projects, he'd worked on *Tonight with Trevor McDonald* and *Stars in their Eyes* and had produced a twelve-part documentary on the eccentric side of American life.

When Charlie called I was frantically busy travelling around doing talks to companies and then racing back to France to be with Shara. I hardly ever had much time in London. But he insisted.

'I'll meet you at Gatwick for a coffee,' he suggested.

I was impressed, and we eventually met at Finnegan's Bar at the airport. I told him about my plan to try to cross the North Atlantic but said I had already made a commitment to another cameraman.

'I've got to be honest with you,' I said. 'This other guy is the most likely to be our cameraman. He's hugely experienced and fired-up and it looks ninety-nine per cent certain that he's going to come along. I'm sorry, buddy, but it's gone.'

Charlie said he understood. 'Just keep me in mind,' he added as we said goodbye.

He rang me every week from then on. 'Any changes?' he would ask ... again.

I'd tell him nothing had changed, and I would hear the disappointment in his voice.

Then, in October 2002, complications arose in the arrangements with our original cameraman, Will Ingham. It became clear that the production company due to film the expedition couldn't now pay him for his time, and at that stage we were in no position to pay him a market-related fee ourselves. The expedition bank account that Nige had helped me set up still had zero in it. Not one measly penny. We couldn't make any sort of commitment to a cameraman now without the support of a production company; I mean, we didn't even have the funds for a lifejacket.

On top of this, something didn't feel quite right. I felt uneasy with the idea of paying anyone to join the expedition. People had to want to be aboard our RIB. It wasn't about the money. This couldn't be a job – I wanted it to be someone's everything.

In that sense Charlie was our man. He was the one who had chased me and chivvied me. I called him soon after Christmas and asked if he was still keen on the idea. It would be unpaid, and would cost him the best part of six months' work. I'd pay for everything for him on the expedition – kit, flights, etc. – but his time and expertise would have to be for free. It was all or nothing.

I promised myself that if he agreed to come under those conditions, I would make it up to him if I could afford it when the time came and would buy him the smartest camera available as a present. In the end, I could afford it – just – and I hope that Charlie's commitment to us paid off for him too. Certainly the money I shelled out on that camera was the best I've spent in a long time.

Just like Nige, Charlie leaped at the chance. He didn't hesitate for a moment. I liked that. He had been determined enough to hunt me down in Chamonix, resolved enough to meet me at Gatwick and gutsy enough to keep asking. It worked.

Charlie might have had little knowledge of the ocean, or much real experience with boats, but he compensated with enthusiasm and grittiness. He was like a sponge, so eager to learn and master new skills. I'd catch him reading books on rough-water boat-handling and asking Nige endless questions about navigating in the fog that we knew would be so prevalent in the Labrador Sea. Whatever it was, he wanted to know – from EPIRB frequencies and emergency call-out procedures to knots and magnetic variations. Above all, he seemed to get a real buzz out of everything.

I remember one specific moment during the sea trials when I looked across the boat and saw him just grinning to himself. He was loving every moment.

Charlie recalls:

I had just got back from Australia, and I heard about Bear's plans. I wanted more than anything to be involved and thought I would give him a call and see what happened. I had no idea what to expect because I had only ever been on a yacht off the coast of Africa, but I just had the feeling it would be amazing.

In selecting Mick, Nige and Charlie, I suppose I had essentially based my choice on character, people I knew well, people in whom I had trust, people who knew me and who I felt would bond together. Really, they were my mates.

The only exception to this rule of thumb was my choice of engineer. There was a brief and pretty desperate period when we thought Mick could be the engineer. This was mainly because he was interested in tractors. Fortunately for all concerned, this folly evaporated like mist in the morning sun when I caught him failing to jump-start his old 1940s tractor down a hill, with clouds of smoke billowing out. 'Mick, I love you,' I told him, 'but we need a professional.'

As the plans gained momentum it became blatantly obvious that for a boat that was going to be single-engined, due to the sheer distance we were going to be travelling and hence the limitations on the amount of fuel we could carry, finding a professional engineer was critical. That one engine would be our lifeline – literally – and without it working, it mattered very little how big and brave our team was.

I wasn't used to having to rely so heavily on machinery – before, it was the human factor that had been critical on high mountains. But this time, keeping that precious sole engine working was going to be the most important job on the expedition. I needed somebody who could keep it working in what would possibly be the worst conditions such an engine had ever been in.

Mick and I had both served in the armed forces, and it became clear that it made sense to try to involve the Royal Navy.

I approached a naval friend, Captain Willie Pennefather. He put me in touch with the navy's PR team, who seemed to get right behind us; and, with the promise of the main front slot at the Schroders London Boat Show assured, we had some pulling power for them as well. But it was more than that. If the expedition proved successful, the navy's involvement would demonstrate its core values of adventure, teamwork and professionalism. So we formed an agreement whereby we would take a Royal Navy engineer with us as one of the crew.

The navy would also help with the berthing of the RIB at the RN Sailing Centre at Portsmouth, under the command of Lieutenant Commander Bill Rothwell. In addition, the navy offered to supply us with 20 tonnes of fuel for the sea-trialling. It was more than I had ever hoped for.

In the end the navy's commitment to us far outweighed even this, and their proactive support was crucial, especially in linking us up with the Danish and Canadian navies, who we knew were the only people who operated the rescue ships up in the Arctic. It was slowly becoming apparent that the naval side of the expedition was fundamental to our chances of success. (That is, of course, if you can manage to restrain the navy boys from taking you out drinking, which bitter experience has taught me is always a bad idea.)

The head of Fleet Corporate Communications, Captain Alistair Halliday, placed an advertisement in the *Navy News*. 'One naval engineer volunteer needed for arduous northerly expedition. Well paid, extra leave, but cold and misery guaranteed, with no ward room to escape the wind and waves!'

We received three replies and prepared to run some form of selection process. The first candidate was Lieutenant Andy Leivers, who came to visit me on our barge in London. He seemed to enjoy the environment, telling Shara she had a lovely galley and referring to our loo as the 'heads'. He was very polite, and very naval.

It was a sunny day, so I suggested Andy and I should take the little RIB that we keep on the Thames out for a spin. I quite often take people down the river and they invariably flounder aboard rather uncomfortably and take some time to settle. Andy was different. He was obviously completely at ease on the water and I remember how precisely and professionally he tidied away the rope, tying a perfect bowline round the stanchion with one hand.

While we were preparing to climb on to the RIB, Shara had been inside the barge, on the phone to her mum. She had heard us clambering around on deck and quickly jumped to conclusions.

'I don't believe it, Mum,' she gasped. 'Bear said he would put these guys through this selection process, and I think he really means it. I can hear them on deck and he's making the Lieutenant do press-ups. Poor guy's dressed in his best trousers!'

Luckily for Andy that wasn't the case. I wasn't that harsh (although I subsequently found out he would have loved to have done some press-ups) and in any case I was quickly becoming convinced that Andy Leivers was exactly the kind of person we needed. He had joined the Royal Navy as a marine apprentice at the age of seventeen, risen through the ranks to become an officer, then read engineering at Southampton University. He was now serving as Deputy Marine Engineer on HMS *Newcastle*. He was eminently qualified, and he seemed fun, diligent and cautious.

I didn't even see the other two candidates.

Andy recalls:

I have my mother to thank first of all, because as an avid *Daily Telegraph* reader, she had read an article by Bear about his forthcoming record attempt across the North Atlantic. The article was titled: 'Is this the frozen limit?' She sent it to me saying it looked up my street and maybe I should apply.

I soon found myself up in London ready for an interview. I got an interview of sorts, but an interview the Bear Grylls way: on an RIB going up the Thames at forty knots! We had a blast and the more I heard about it all, the more I began to get seriously excited about the prospect of joining the team.

I knew Andy was the right guy. So we worked out a deal with Captain Halliday, whereby Andy would essentially be seconded to us from the Royal Navy.

I sought two assurances from the navy: the first was that they would allow Andy to be 100 per cent committed to our expedition and would not call him away for other duties or operations. I felt it was essential for Andy to understand that if the men he had been in charge of were sent to Iraq, or elsewhere, his commitment was still to be to this expedition. I understood how hard this might be for him if war broke out. They were his men, whom he'd looked after. But he knew what I was after and agreed. As it transpired, his men were used in coping with the fire service strikes at home, and not in the Gulf, so Andy really only missed an alternative way of getting soaked.

The second assurance I needed from the navy was that they would support me as leader of this expedition and I would have the authority of the navy behind me if I needed it. I felt it was important to lay this down early and for Andy to know he was on secondment and that I was in charge.

Both these conditions were agreed.

I was immensely relieved to have pulled this off. It was a huge deal for us. I felt tremendously privileged to have secured the services of a first-rate engineer from the finest navy in the world.

Through the weeks that followed, I became increasingly impressed by Andy's professionalism. He took total responsibility for the engine and fuel systems, and regularly brought me charts indicating how we could maximize the boat's performance. Cautious by nature and conservative in his analysis, he seemed to provide the ideal counterbalance to me. But on top of this, I reckoned that he was the kind of person who would help me make the right decisions under pressure in the middle of the ocean.

Mick had really pushed me to involve the Royal Navy somehow. He felt that it provided important security. He said that if the navy were just 'sponsors' and it all went wrong, they might be less inclined to send out the search-and-rescue than if we had one of their personnel on board. I agreed; but it was more than that. We now had an engineer who had been trained to the highest level, a man who also had a real understanding of the sea, weather and fuel management. And I knew that the more knowledge we had on this little boat, the better.

Finally, Andy came across as a kind man. I didn't want somebody who was just super-strong and super-confident in whatever they did. It was as important to me that I found someone who would work through a tough night and then be kind enough to offer you the roll-mat at the end. And Andy was exactly that sort of person.

So this was the crew: Mick, Nige, Charlie and Andy. I was convinced of their individual qualities, and hopeful we would bond together well. But there is always an element of the unknown and probably the most intense few months of our lives lay ahead.

But that bonding did come. And I remember when it happened.

It was one evening, not long before we left for Canada, when the whole team were together, meticulously going through each stage of the route point by point. At the start, this type of meeting had been dominated by me, talking them through all the plans, but this time it was different. They were all talking, buried in maps, fuel-ratio diagrams, wave-chart data, Danish naval emergency procedures, call signs, you name it. They talked about stuff I didn't even understand. It was fantastic. I just sat quietly and watched. I could sense in their voices the anticipation of what lay ahead. This was their expedition as much as it was mine. We were all in this together now.

This was what I had always wanted. I smiled to myself and opened a bottle of wine.

'To the times ahead,' I said, raising a glass.

'To the times ahead,' they replied, hardly even looking up as they continued poring over the charts.

This was my team. I knew I'd got lucky.

3. COUNTDOWN

Fall down seven times. Get up eight.

Japanese proverb

One glance at the long list of sponsors provided at the end of this book might create the impression that this was one of the most effortlessly funded expeditions in the history of exploration.

It wasn't.

In truth, the expedition was originally scheduled for the summer of 2002 but had to be postponed because we hadn't raised enough money. In fact, after two years we had still raised no money. Nothing at all.

I think people often assume that the world of expeditions is glamorous and romantic, but the reality is very different. Most of the actual expeditions themselves involve being continually cold, wet and frightened. And any notions of 'romance' tend to dissipate pretty quickly when the temperature drops below freezing and stays there. Whereas in the movies it is all OK again two hours later, the bottom line for us is that two hours later you are still there – no change, still cold, still wet and still frightened.

The other reality of an expedition is that 90 per cent of your time is spent in the preparation. And for us that preparation time was two years of uncertainty and self-doubt. As rejection letters poured in as quickly as the proposals were dispatched, I questioned myself constantly: 'Why is this not working?'

I struggled every day to find an answer.

When you put all your being into something afresh each morning, and it continually gets thrown back in your face, it's hard. But life is rarely easy. And the bottom line is that we eventually reached our target only because we were bloody-minded enough to keep going.

So many times people advised me to accept reality and try something else, and there were definitely moments when I thought they might be right. Day after day, the arrival of an envelope with a company logo would provoke a surge of excitement, but this was invariably followed by deep frustration when I read the politely worded but negative response. Month after month, it was the same. But somehow I found it even harder to give up; instead, I just became difficult to live with.

Nige and I dispatched literally hundreds of proposals in the course of two years, all neatly printed and bound. We raised absolutely nothing, although there were a few moments when we glimpsed success.

Our initial strategy was to seek one overall title sponsor who would take all the commercial benefits on offer in return for the sum of £250,000. This, we hoped, would be the knockout punch: the one big deal that would fund the expedition and end our worries.

For many months, these hugely optimistic right hooks kept missing the target. Then, just as hope was fading, British

Telecom appeared to be moving within range. They seemed genuinely interested and we were invited to make a presentation at their offices in Ipswich. Mick and Nige took an afternoon off work and we drove up there together. We soon found ourselves standing in BT's huge boardroom and we gave it our all. But it soon became clear they couldn't write that size of cheque. It was just too much. So the bargaining began.

After some time they asked: 'Do you think you could do it for £90,000?'

'Well, yes . . . just,' I replied.

After so many rejections, I would have accepted anything. All I wanted was to do the expedition, and there in the BT boardroom we started to calculate how we could do it for £90,000, how much we could save if we bought a second-hand boat, cut back on this piece of kit and scrimped on communications. Deep down I knew it was madness.

Thankfully, in the end, BT said no, and our bank balance remained at zero. If they had, and we had gone ahead with a cut-price expedition, we would have seriously compromised our safety. It would have been sacrificing a safety margin that we already didn't have.

The explorer Sir Ranulph Fiennes once said, 'Staying the course is what counts – them that stick it out is them that win.' I had read this in a magazine, saved the cutting and tucked it just inside the frame of the mirror in our bedroom. I read it all the time. But, mentally, we were in the trenches. Sponsorship is always a process of attrition but I felt I was losing. It was clear that we needed a fresh approach.

Robert Swan is another man I really admire. He has led expeditions to both the North and South Poles, and had become a friend. We had bought our barge from him in London, and his old boat was now our home. Rob is a good man and one I respect. He just quietly gets on with things, and does them well. I like that. Around this time, I bumped into him at a lecture at the Royal Geographical Society one balmy summer evening. We cut away from the crowds who were milling around drinking afterwards, and sat on the steps in the garden. I needed his advice and some help. I soon knew that what he was telling me was like gold dust.

He said that rather than seek one overall sponsor, we should just create smaller, simpler packages and look for a larger number of sponsors. It seemed too obvious. 'Make it manageable,' he continued. 'You have a whole host of companies whose conferences you've spoken at, who like what you do. They'll buy into this dream if it's less money and justifiable.' I listened carefully. 'Offer them a free talk and a day out on the boat afterwards and for £15,000, rather than £250,000, they have the branding and a simple way for their staff to feel part of the adventure.'

He was absolutely right.

For a company to write a cheque for £250,000, not only do they need the approval of the board, but the timing has to be perfect and the proposal must match all their corporate values, etc. That's not always easy. It is much simpler for them to write out a cheque for £15,000 if it gives them a way of keeping involved with what you are doing and benefits the staff internally as much as the exposure does externally. 'All you have to do,' Rob concluded, 'is find twelve companies who will take this kind of package.'

So I did as he advised, to the letter. We created these new £15,000 packages and sent them to everyone again. But somehow the rejections still poured in.

I couldn't understand why.

I sent out more.

Then one day in September 2002, we suffered particularly heavy losses. Four rejections arrived in the same post, all from key companies I had targeted. 'I can't believe they've said "no",' I muttered to myself out of frustration. 'Those were my best hopes.' I was confused. I held my head in my hands. Nima, our dog, came over and sat on my feet as she often did. Then I heard a voice from outside the door. 'Bear, are you OK?'

It was one of our neighbours on the quay, Heidi-Jane Smith.

Our barge is one of ten house-boats moored at the same pier on the Thames, and I live there for one reason. In this big, faceless city we have something special: a community. People care and tend to look out for one another. It makes coming home so good.

I told Heidi things were not going well, and she listened.

'Well,' she said after a while, 'why don't you give me one of your proposals? I can't promise anything, but I will give it to the people at work, at Vitol, and we'll see what happens.'

The following day I saw Heidi again. She was smiling as she banged on the door.

'They'll do it,' she said as I opened the hatch.

'What?'

'We'll take one of the £15,000 packages. Vitol have said they will be a sponsor.'

I could hardly believe it. I literally picked Heidi up and squeezed her. After so many months of people saying no, someone was actually saying yes. Vitol, an oil-marketing company, had become our first sponsor. That night, I started working out if we could do the expedition on only £15,000.

We were off the mark.

Not long afterwards, Lunson Mitchenall, the company of property surveyors that Nige works for, also agreed to take one of the packages. That news sent me scampering off again to calculate whether we could make it now with just £30,000. It was beginning to happen. Yes by yes, our hopes and expectations started to gain ground. Then Shell agreed, then Lafarge Aggregates. Even BT came back. It was afford-able now.

We had found a formula and it was working: the more talks I found myself doing, the more I would follow them up with a proposal. And people just got it; it was simple and justifiable and it made sense. My belief in it grew, and com-panies sensed that. There was a momentum behind us now.

In the end we filled all the lead sponsor slots within two months. In total a dozen companies, from General Motors in Canada to the *Daily Telegraph* over here in the UK, took the £15,000 package, and we still had the title sponsorship to sell.

We were prepared to name the entire project after one

company, in all the press coverage and branding. It would include the boat's name, the title logos, talks and corporate days afterwards, and this bundle was going to cost someone £50,000.

Early in 2003, just before the Boat Show, I learned that a Swiss–British company, British Masters, a specialist watch-making group, was trying to contact me through a speakers' agency. They had read an article on 'risk' I had done in the *Daily Telegraph* and they had liked it. But more importantly, they saw an opportunity. The company was headed up by a couple of Swiss guys from Lausanne, Eric Loth and Jean-Marie Florent, and when I contacted them, they explained they were eager to revive a connection with British exploration which the company had developed in the days of Shackleton and Scott. They had a brand they wanted to relaunch world-wide – it was called Arnold and Son.

'Well,' I replied, 'the title sponsorship is still available, and . . .' I paused, then I just went for it . . . 'if you can make your mind up within the next forty-eight hours, we will have time to get the boat covered in Arnold and Son logos by the time it appears at the London Boat Show in three weeks' time. It could be amazing.'

Some time before, I had agreed with the organizers of the Boat Show at Earl's Court to display our boat on a podium at the front of the exhibition. It was the same place where Sir Francis Chichester's *Gypsy Moth* had stood during the Boat Show in 1967. I felt honoured and also a little daunted, but I knew it was the chance of a lifetime. We just ran with it.

Arnold and Son instantly recognized the opportunity. They wanted to call us the 'Arnold and Son Trans Atlantic Arctic Expedition'. It was a bit of a mouthful and took me seven attempts to say fluently on our answer-machine, but it was really happening now. They called back the following day to say they would like to take the title sponsorship slot at £50,000. We had never met in person and we agreed all this on our word alone. That was it, and it was a great way to cement a deal.

Their corporate logos went to print, and the first time we met was on a freezing January morning outside the Boat Show. There was snow on the ground, and the partially completed boat stood proudly at an angle, floodlit for all to see. When Eric and Jean-Marie saw it, they smiled to themselves. She was perfect. We knew we had been given our final break, and we had sufficient funding to set up the expedition just as we wanted. We were truly up and running.

Both the boat-builders and I had bust a gut to get everything ready in time for the show, and together we had done it. It had gone to the wire and a whole team of people were helping late into the night before the show opened.

The logos were sealed round the base of the stand, the maps waterproofed and sealed to the sides, and a Musto mannequin, dressed in full survival suit, was perched on the half-finished tubes of the hull, high above the ground. It gave the whole boat life. Each night before I left for home, I patted her hull. She was to be our home and our only lifeline out there in the ice-strewn seas. Sitting there silhouetted at night, with the hull covered in the signatures of so many well-wishers, she was already looking beautiful.

I was exhausted though, and so was Shara. She had seen her carefully maintained home slowly become buried under a mountain of equipment, logos and survival gear. Even Christmas had been a washout of phone calls and late nights. I tried desperately to keep home as home, but it never quite happened. By New Year Shara was four months pregnant and was still trying to help me. But I could tell she was drained.

She had been pregnant earlier in the year but it hadn't worked out for us. Shara had been distraught. As I held her in my arms, sobbing in the hospital, I knew we had just lost everything we had ever hoped for together. But what broke my heart even more was seeing her pain. Her miscarriage left us both feeling empty.

Life had thrown us some bitter deals. Within two years of marriage, we had both lost our fathers, Shara's dad, Brian, having passed away only ten weeks before mine. We had cried in bed together for so many nights since. Her getting pregnant was a way forward. But then we lost it. Life was sick. And we were struggling. I just felt this ache inside. But Shara was incredibly strong and, like so many women before her, she quietly and slowly picked herself up and carried on. She was truly an inspiration.

Six months later, she was pregnant again. But this time she was terrified. As I held her each morning, with her hand in mine, and felt her caress her tummy nervously, I promised her everything would be OK. She'd close her eyes and say she believed me.

Deep down, I knew that this next year was going to change everything. I prayed to God I wouldn't let her down.

4. FIRST BLOOD

The world often steps aside for people who
know where they're going.

Miriam Viola Larsen

So the money was finally raised, and a myth developed in exploration circles that I had, somehow, discovered the secret of securing sponsorship to fund an expedition. Many people have contacted me since to ask for advice, perhaps thinking I have an address book full of contacts just waiting to write cheques. I wish that was true. In fact the secret was nothing more glamorous than that Ranulph Fiennes quote which so simply said, 'them that stick it out is them that win'.

As time went by, I became increasingly grateful that the Royal Navy was on board, and I recognized that its level of involvement and enthusiasm owed much to the contacts and help of Captain Willie Pennefather.

I had first met Willie a year earlier. We had started talking about the sea and I told him about my hopes for this North Atlantic crossing. He was hugely enthusiastic about it all, and in no time I began to recognize his expertise. Ever since that evening, and particularly since my father died, he has been somebody whom I can trust and turn to; someone whom I can be sure has my best interests at heart. That means a lot to me.

He used his access to the highest echelons of the Royal Navy and eloquently explained why he thought it should get involved in our project. The First Sea Lord agreed, and doors began to swing open.

Beyond this, we had Willie as a constant and reliable source of support and advice. With his experience and contacts, he was the ideal man to stand quietly in the background, ready and willing to make the vital decisions at crucial moments, and in this decisive role he would in time prove absolutely invaluable.

I asked Willie to speak at the naming ceremony of the boat, on 29 April 2003 down in Portsmouth, and he used the opportunity to explain why he felt so strongly about this expedition.

You will all know what the challenge is – it is to cross the Atlantic by the Arctic route in an open, rigid inflatable boat some ten metres long, through some of the most testing conditions and waters that the Almighty has made available to people like Bear Grylls and his team . . .

Quite mad, I hear you say, but is it? Yes, it's all about endurance and achievement, but, more importantly, it's about the team. The bonds you create in those extremes. The sea offers an abundance of opportunity for challenge, but also for belonging, and so often I have seen it transform nervous, under-confident people into fulfilled team players. Men with a much greater and enduring purpose in life.

Such adventurers as these are an inspiration to us all. It takes guts and imagination, and often a short memory, to delve into the unknown. Often, management accounts and targets tend to dominate today, but these count for nothing if we lose our spirit. It is this spirit that these adventurers stir in us all. They bring joy and smiles to people's faces and they fire up something that often lurks too far beneath the surface in the rest of us.

The adventurers are the ones who show opportunity to others, through their visible determination to risk everything, to have a go, and through their determination to succeed.

Bear, I can't tell you what a tremendous honour it was for me when you asked me to speak at the naming of your boat, your pride and joy, and the First Sea Lord has asked me to say that the navy much admires your values and is thrilled to have been able to help and take part in the expedition under your leadership.

Good luck, God bless, and above all come home safe and sound.

The combined effect of finally having money in the bank and the navy on our side gave enormous impetus to our preparations, but the single most significant consequence of these developments was that we could afford to build exactly the kind of boat that we wanted to take into these precarious, icy waters.

I first came across Ocean Dynamics when I was casually browsing through a trade boating magazine and noticed their small advertisement in the classified section. They sold themselves as specialists in building tough, resilient boats, and when we saw they made lifeboats for the RNLI (Royal National Lifeboat Institute), worked with clients in Scandinavia and didn't do too many drinks trays, we sensed we had found the right people to build our boat.

They were based at Pembroke docks, far away in west Wales, so Mick, Nige and I drove five hours from London and found ourselves sitting in a Portakabin describing the boat we needed.

Shaun White and his team listened patiently. We said we wanted a boat with a range of 1,000 miles, and we needed extreme durability; we wanted an aluminium hull that wouldn't crack if it hit small, submerged icebergs at night, and we needed a jet engine instead of a propeller that, again, wouldn't get damaged by hitting any floating debris or random containers. None of us wanted to spend the amount of time and energy preparing as we had and then find ourselves 500 miles offshore without a prop, having clipped something in the night. It was a risk we could minimize and it made sense to give ourselves the best advantage at this early stage.

Other boat-builders had considered our requirements but said we were asking for the impossible. It was too difficult, too risky. So we looked again. These men didn't say that, but they quickly and bluntly identified our main challenge as finding a way to carry the required amount of fuel in an efficient manner.

'I think it's possible . . .' Shaun White said, smiling.

That was what we wanted to hear.

Through all the deliberations and discussions that followed, as we pored over power ratios, different types of engine and various configurations of storing the fuel, we accepted professional advice when it was given and constantly focused our efforts on minimizing the expedition's technical risks.

Shaun became a friend and a confidant and I ended up

calling him, 'Uncle'. The name has stuck. When we finally came to leave, Shaun was determined to be there with us in Nova Scotia. He flew out with us and looked so proud as hundreds of well-wishers looked round the boat on the quay-side in Halifax. It had been his baby too, and he had put his heart and soul into its construction. Part of me wished 'Uncle Shaun' was coming with us as well.

Difficult decisions were unavoidable in the design phase, because we were going into new territory with the specifi-cation. For example, the ideal would have been to fit two engines, but with the range we needed there simply was not room for double the fuel load. Our need for fuel economy meant we could have only one engine. I know Andy was taken aback when he saw this arrangement because it left us with no fallback option – the navy follows the belt-and-braces principle where you make sure you always have a Plan B – but RIBs are generally designed to have a range of around 100, not 1,000, miles. It was a risk we had no choice in taking.

Even to achieve this kind of extended range, we needed to carry 4,000 litres of fuel and the reality was that we could go further by using one engine rather than two. That was the bottom line.

The question of how to store the fuel occupied the team's minds for a long time. We knew the performance of the boat would be poor at the start of each leg because we would be so heavy with fuel, but we had to try to ensure the weight was spread as economically as possible across the boat. It would be a deciding factor in really heavy seas. Move two tonnes of weight and it makes a huge difference to the trim and pitch of the boat. I was forced to sit back and let the experts work out these different ratios – my job was to probe, to question and then to trust their decisions.

Andy was coming into his own now. He was brilliant in this area, and as soon as he joined the team full-time I took real confidence from his presence in all these vital early discussions. He was diligent and exact, and he was cautious and conservative by nature: vital ingredients in a craft where we were dependent on only one engine.

As soon as the boat was ready, we began to plan the sea trials. These were always going to be critical. We had been designing a boat that was in many ways unique. No one really knew how she would perform fully laden in a swell. Only our trials would tell us that. We needed to test and trial at different payloads in different conditions, and then retest. A thousand miles was already at our outermost limit of range. If we got these small calculations wrong, it could be critical.

We also needed to trial the human factor; how we, the team, would cope. Living in what was described by one journalist as 'an area the size of an open-top car' for over 3,000 miles of wild seas, with no shelter, strapped in day after day, would take its toll on us physically. We needed to begin to get used to her and learn how to feel at home on board.

My plan was that these trials should be short and focused, intensive weekends when the team would be on the boat, seeing what worked, what didn't, getting used to the way she handled and finding out how we would cope when it cut rough.

There was a balance to be found: we had to get a reasonable number of miles on the engine and get the early services out of the way before we set out on the ocean but, on the other hand, I didn't want any of us to be sick and tired of the boat by the time we reached Canada. It still needed to be fresh and exciting.

So, for the first sea trial weekend, we planned to take the boat from Portsmouth to the Scilly Isles and back. The weather was not great and within an hour or so of the start most of us were feeling sick. I had forgotten quite how debilitating seasickness can be. You fix your eyes on the horizon, but that doesn't stop the world inside you starting to spin. We would need an endless supply of anti-seasickness pills.

We learned lessons, and took notes.

We would have to wear our helmets when the sea was rough, to protect our heads if we fell or slipped as we shifted around the boat. Pot Noodles made us vomit. Talcum powder needed to be at hand to ease the gradual biting of the neck and wrist seals of the dry-suits into our skin. Vaseline protected our nostrils from the salt and spray and prevented them becoming raw.

The idea of having an inflatable mattress in the 'sardine tin', the area at the back of the boat where two, maybe three of us, could lie down and rest, seemed inspired. It wasn't. The mattress made us feel sick and was easily punctured. OK, so we needed to get some absorbent foam instead.

We hadn't planned where we would put our feet when we were helming, so they dangled uncomfortably in mid-air. Right, we would need to weld some kind of footrest into position.

The boat, in the final stages of building, became a test bed for many maritime companies. Many people approached us with new ideas. Some were bonkers; some were amazing.

By the end we were trialling seats for the new naval fast-response crafts, testing a small exterior water heater that would take the pounding of all poundings and only worked periodically. We were also experimenting with a marine tracking device that would send back a signal every half-hour with our speed and latitude and longitude, as given by the GPS (Global Positioning System). This data was sent via satellite to the Internet and became a lifeline to those waiting for news back in the UK. But it had its dangers too, and when all our systems went down in a storm, including this device, people understandably jumped to conclusions. They would see our speed gradually falling away and the weather patterns worsening. When we went blank and offline, we were in trouble, but it wasn't fatal. We were still upright, but they weren't to know.

Yet when it worked, it gave people hope; hope that slowly we were coming home, wave by wave.

By the end of that first night of our sea trial, we were all starting to feel really cold, which was not promising. This was a midsummer's night off the south coast of England, not the frozen North Atlantic. We weren't even that wet, but it became obvious we were going to need much more kit if we weren't to freeze. But already we were looking like Michelin men in all our gear.

More notes were made.

The wind always whistled behind us wherever we sat and we lost a lot of heat like this; roll-mats to sit on would shield our backsides.

We needed better lifelines: the clips were far too small – in a storm at night, in mittens, we'd never get clipped on. They needed to run the whole length of the boat, and be big and strong.

These were all small details but, in my experience, on any expedition it is the small things that make the biggest difference. Something that seems insignificant and minor on shore can make a life-altering difference at sea, so I was determined that every little glitch and problem should be identified and resolved at this stage. When we finally left, it would be too late for this sort of refinement. This was the time to iron things out, when it was calm and when it was good, before it got nasty.

The truth is that our first night aboard the boat had not been much fun and, weighed down by fuel and hindered by rough weather, we had not made very good progress towards the Scilly Isles. We were all tired and wet, so at four in the morning it seemed sensible to tie up on a buoy at Salcombe harbour in Devon. Our performance might not have been outstanding, but it was our first time out and there was no point in going completely mad. We waited until dawn, then headed off to find some breakfast on shore.

I had spoken to Neil Laughton, the leader of our Everest expedition, during the previous week and knew he was planning to be in the Salcombe area over the weekend. We bumped into him in the village and he casually asked if we could take him and a couple of friends out for a spin on the water.

'No problem,' I replied; it would be fun, just like the old days. We were laughing and joking. The mood was good. Neil was excited to see the boat.

Somewhere in the dark recesses of my mind, however, a bell was ringing. I remembered that Salcombe was known for a raised strip of sand and rock just beneath the water's surface, somewhere near the front of the harbour. 'Salcombe Bar', as it is called, was reputed to be one of the most treacherous hazards on the British coastline.

The conditions were wind over tide now. Later – too late – I read the view of a round-the-world yachtsman who said he had seen awkward conditions all around the globe but nothing quite so bad as the Salcombe Bar.

But this was only a muffled bell at the back of my mind as we headed out into the harbour. Neil was standing right at the bow of the boat, with two of his friends, and all seemed well. I did notice the waves were beginning to build just a bit, but everybody was relaxed and smiling, shooting the breeze.

Then I looked straight ahead and saw what can only be described as a monster wave approaching. It was probably around 200 yards away, but it was very obviously heading in our direction.

Standing at the helm, my first instinct was to turn the boat and run away from this thing. Then I decided there was not enough time. We would have to face the wave head-on and try to ride it. Seconds passed like minutes. Nobody was laughing any more. This rogue wave rolled irrepressibly towards us. People grabbed at handholds. We were doing only 10 knots.

It connected head-on, and our boat literally took off, nose up, out of the water. Then we dropped straight down 15 feet as the wave fell with a crash on to the stern of the boat. She pitched forward wildly. It felt as though we had all been standing in an elevator and the cable had broken, and we had fallen down two storeys and smashed into the bottom.

Andy gashed his knee. I was shaking like a leaf. Neil was still just clinging on.

'You guys are insane,' he said, smiling, after we had turned the boat round and run back to shore with the subsequent waves. 'You wouldn't catch me 500 miles offshore in this thing, in a big sea. Bloody hell! It'll be nuts.'

To be honest, my legs were still shaking a couple of hours later, but in time we would learn to deal with waves like that. It was a matter of confidence and trust. We were learning how to handle her in these conditions, slowly but surely, day by day.

On our second sea trial, we encountered some similar

conditions around Portland Bill, Dorset, when the sea was breaking up and coming at us wildly from every direction. The area was infamous for its rough waters. Although it was only a small taste of what we would find out in the big ocean, we began to feel the boat responding really well to the challenge. It was what she was designed for and she loved it.

Andy was handling the throttle, I was helming and the boat was alive. We were being thrown around, but we were making progress, finding our way, starting to enjoy the challenge. The adrenalin was up.

The following day, with everyone back at work, each of the guys – Mick, Nige, Charlie and Andy – called me individually to say they could hardly move because of the physical battering they had taken on the water. I felt it too. We were stiff and sore, and that was after only fifteen hours in no more than tricky conditions.

Our early trials left us in no doubt about the scale and nature of what lay ahead. Legs of almost 900 miles over several days would leave us battered and bruised, and that worried me. I was wiped out after only a day and a night – in summertime.

It became increasingly obvious that the real challenge for us was the fact that we were in a completely open boat, with nowhere to hide. I had underestimated this. In a round-the-world yacht you have a cabin where you can shelter from the worst of the weather, a place to get out of the rain and spray, a place to rest and get dry in. We had no such luxury, no respite from the elements. Whatever the weather and sea conditions, whether it was rain, sleet, waves, hail or spray, this was where we would live, eat and sleep. It was to become our most exhausting factor: the relentless wet, cold and exposure. And we all learned to dread it.

For our final sea trial, we travelled the 90 or so miles from Portsmouth to Jersey and back. We took the time to run through all our safety procedures: deploying the life raft, putting out the parachute sea anchor, rehearsing our 'man-overboard' drills. It wasn't the same as the real thing, but these were necessary disciplines to have learnt by heart. Being able to deploy the sea anchor in under two minutes as waves pounded over the foredeck at night had to be instinctive; and that takes time to learn.

I threw endless fenders overboard for the guys to retrieve, all of us learning how to handle the boat delicately in a pitching sea. I did it again at dusk. They were getting it.

By 3 a.m., Mick was on watch. Everyone was tired. It was time for a live test of the 'man-overboard' drill; I had decided to be the dummy, and I wasn't looking forward to it. I was lying in the sardine tin with Nige, unable to sleep. I looked anxiously at my watch. We were exactly mid-Channel now. It was the worst time on the worst shift. I sat up, gave Nige a nudge just to make sure he was awake, stood on the tubes and jumped into the black.

As per the drills, everyone leaped into action and Mick brought the boat round into the sea. The spotlight flickered on and they soon had me in the lee of the RIB, Mick carefully balancing the jet controls holding me off by 5 yards.

'What's it worth, skipper?' he shouted into the night. I was cold now and my heart was still pounding. I laughed, but only a little.

'England is sixty miles that-a-way,' he chuckled. 'See you for breakfast.' He drove off.

A short dogleg, and he was back alongside me.

'Mick, you've got ten seconds to bring me in or I *will* kill you.' Strong hands dragged me in, floundering. Andy threw me one of his diesel rags to dry myself, laughing. But it had been a good drill to do.

The night was perfect, the sea was still and the stars and sky were bright. It was as easy as pie. We all sat quietly afterwards and could only imagine what it would be like in a wind-whipped gale with icebergs all around. It would be a different game altogether. The truth is that getting back to a man overboard would be near impossible, and we all knew it. We turned and headed for home.

In many ways, the expedition was beginning to assume its own momentum. The funds were in the bank; the boat-building process was finally complete. We were talking to shipping agents, managing relationships with sponsors, discussing finer details of the route and working out possible dates of departure bearing in mind the state of the ice-packs in the Arctic and the weather patterns coming in. We were busier than ever.

There had been times, especially in the early days, when it had sometimes felt as though the entire expedition was resting on my shoulders. It was my dream and I was struggling to make it happen. Those days had gone now, and most of the time I was able to stand back and oversee all the activity. I loved that.

Everything was happening all around me.

We had arranged two major crew meetings before the expedition, one six months before our scheduled departure and one just a week before. Every aspect of the expedition was discussed and checked. Nige had all his maps laid out and carefully went over the routes and the contingency plans once again; Andy talked about the engine and the refuelling requirements; Mick went over the emergency coastguard procedures and weather plans, and Chloë distributed her logistics folders.

Chloë Boyes was working for Goldman Sachs in London when we met. I told her one evening, as we chatted after a talk I had given, about the administrative challenges – to put it mildly – that existed in my life. Shara was pregnant, everything was hectic and I was struggling to stay afloat.

She saw the problem as clearly as I did. I needed some help. More than this, she proposed a solution; she wanted some excitement and I wanted an efficient number two. I should employ her as a PA to handle all the admin. I felt a burden lift off me.

It was always going to be hard for me to trust somebody enough to allow them to liaise with the people who provided my living: the CEOs of the companies who use me as a speaker, or the sponsors and contacts surrounding the expedition. But it didn't take long for me to feel comfortable with Chloë in this role.

She was easygoing and efficient and her impact was immediate. It meant the world to me to be able to have the occasional relaxed evening at home with Shara, rather than working late into the night catching up on an inbox full of emails.

Chloë's role within the expedition soon became a vital one. She was going to operate our base from London and the expedition HQ was moved to the offices of Liaison Media, our PR guys, only 100 yards away from our barge. It worked perfectly and was always a hub of banter and fun, the rooms piled high with radios, maps and logos.

I wanted to keep the barge clear for Shara. The London base was going to be our first point of contact with the outside world. Day or night, when we needed help out there, Chloë and that office were to be our lifeline. It was a big responsibility for her.

Most of the crew didn't know much about her to start with, but as soon as she handed out her neatly prepared folders, packed with logistics and contact numbers, at our meeting, they started to recognize the importance of her role.

Perhaps the best measure of her enormous contribution was the fact that as soon as we finally reached Scotland, Mick, Nige, Charlie and Andy all told me they wanted to get her something special to say thank you; thank you for those times she was there for us, coordinating and crisis-managing situations in real time. They all chipped in to buy her a glass and silver bowl, engraved with the words 'for always being there'.

Chloë had teamed up with our PR company, Liaison Media, which was headed up by a real live-wire of a guy called Alex Rayner. When Alex had first heard about our expedition he had suggested he become involved, and had been immensely excited from day one. And it showed. 'Ha,' he would announce, having arranged another interview for one of us, 'I just love this.' And off he would go.

The final member of our base team was Andy Billing. He had agreed to build a website for the expedition, at minimal cost, and to keep it constantly updated, streaming information as we went along. In the early days we were getting four hits a day, and that was probably me checking to see if anyone was visiting the site. However, during the expedition, as the dramas unfolded, we were registering more than 30,000 hits every day. Andy was in his element. He was so enthusiastic, always obliging and above all professional. And everyone loved it whenever he appeared with his customary greeting: 'Good morning, fine sirs!'

Shara had decided she didn't want to be alone in London while I was away. I agreed with her. She and Jesse would be much happier with her mother out of London. It would be quieter. Andy agreed to live on our barge for the entire duration of the expedition: manning the phones by night.

Just knowing he was always there to help Chloë and answer the telephone gave me the reassurance we all felt we needed. This was the final piece of the jigsaw.

In 2001 I was invited to become an ambassador for the Prince's Trust. It was a huge honour and in return I promised that our next expedition would be in aid of the charity. Ever since then, through various events I have been involved with, I have seen at first hand how effectively and genuinely the Trust provides thousands of young people in Britain with both the incentive and the opportunity to build their dreams. It gives them a chance to get out there and do the very best they can, to start businesses, to find work. It offers a break to people who would never normally get the chance. It is a brilliant idea and it changes lives.

I wrote to HRH The Prince of Wales, the founder of the charity, to explain that we would like his Trust to become our official beneficiary; I also asked if he might ever consider becoming the patron of our expedition. He not only agreed to take on this role but also expressed the desire to meet the entire team before our departure. I couldn't believe it.

On the appointed day, at the appointed time, smartly dressed in our expedition fleeces, we gathered at the barge and hailed a couple of taxis to take us to St James's Palace. I had also invited the two top execs from Arnold and Son, our title sponsors, Eric and Jean-Marie, as a small additional gesture of thanks to them for their support. They looked immaculate, dressed in their suits.

The Prince had obviously been well briefed, and as he entered the room he walked towards me and started to mime the act of spraying deodorant under his arms. He was taking the mickey out of me already, as I had recently featured in the Sure for Men deodorant TV commercials.

'How is the deodorant?' he asked playfully.

'It's fine, thank you, sir,' I replied awkwardly.

Then, after a moment of silence, I added, 'Well . . .' I paused, 'at least I wasn't asked to do an advert for Anusol.'

My impromptu reference to a remedy for haemorrhoids prompted a rapid shuffling of feet behind me from the guys, but the Prince laughed and the ice was broken. He then told us how during his naval career he had served on a frigate in the North Atlantic. He had encountered a storm so ferocious and powerful that the force of the waves had literally bent a reinforced steel ladder. He looked at me intently.

'And you're going up there in a small rubber-tubed boat. What will you do in that kind of sea?' he asked.

I paused awkwardly.

'We'll call you for some advice when that happens, sir, rest assured,' I replied. There was more shuffling behind me.

He asked Nige how his astral navigation was coming along, and Nige admitted it was something of a grey area. The Prince laughed out loud. The atmosphere was light and fun, and we had some photographs of us all taken outside afterwards.

'Well, I think you're all insane,' the Prince concluded as he turned to leave, 'but I'll be thinking of you.'

As the final day of departure drew nearer, inevitably there were several last-minute crises that needed to be solved in a hurry. At one point Andy Leivers called to say he needed a particular seal for the jet housing. If we couldn't get this specific part quickly, plus a spare, the boat would not be able to leave for Canada, and we would suffer the consequences of that delay. The ice was fragmenting now in the Arctic. The timing was perfect; we had no room for such a delay.

I was making a speech for Fujitsu on that particular morning, and I recall being backstage, all dressed up in my Everest climbing kit, waiting to go on. But I had to make the call to make sure we got this seal, and I had to make it now. I was literally phoning the jet manufacturers when the master of ceremonies stood up to introduce me.

'Can you get the part to the naval yard for tomorrow?' I asked in hushed tones.

'Yes, we can, if I get it sent this morning,' said the voice of Martin Jackson, their marketing director, on the line.

'Thanks, Martin. You're a star. I've got to go. I'm onstage in five seconds. Bye.'

I took a deep breath and walked out onstage to another sea of faces. I was sweating already.

My two lives had almost overlapped, but luckily not quite collided.

The long-running debate over how we would store the fuel reached a critical stage only two weeks before the boat was due to leave. It slowly dawned on us over the final trials that if we were to get the necessary mileage and range, we would need to install an extra fuel bladder under the front deck of the boat. The area was meant to be our storage for food and supplies, but would have to be sacrificed.

The problem was that this particular piece of specialist equipment had a list price of £15,000, and we didn't have that sort of money left in the budget. It was a huge problem to be faced with so late, and it threatened to hold up the entire effort.

I called one company, explained the situation, gave them the sales patter, and they responded by offering us a £500 discount on the fifteen grand. That was kind – of course, they were not obliged to offer us anything at all – but I needed a better deal. In desperation I called the best company in the UK at designing such bladders, specialist suppliers to the armed forces and much, much more expensive than £15,000. I phoned one of the directors at FPT Industries.

This time I simply told them what we were trying to do, what had happened and how desperate we were for help.

'OK, we'll be happy to help,' said Mark Butler, the CEO.

He immediately dispatched a couple of his specialists to see the boat at the naval base in Portsmouth, and, over the next few days, in constant contact with Andy, FPT Industries completed an intensely intricate and professional job.

The fuel bladder they fitted was custom-made from Kevlar, the bullet-proof and flame-resistant material they use to make fuel bladders for fighter planes. Nobody could say they weren't thorough! It was carefully moulded under the bow by a team of experts, plus Andy, and all for no charge at all. I was so grateful. At the final hurdle they had bust a gut, put other orders on hold and cleared the way for us. They made me promise one thing: that we would 'come home safe'.

Such generosity, such professional services so freely given, amazed me time and time again. I was deeply touched by the many companies, and indeed individuals, telling us that if we needed any help at all, we only had to ask.

Perhaps this spirit originates from the maritime culture that if anyone is ever in trouble on the sea, ships in the vicinity will always offer assistance. It is a great culture and is one of the great strengths of the climbing world as well: when lives are on the line, people drop everything to help.

As Captain Pennefather told us afterwards, the whole expedition grew to be much more than an attempt to complete a crossing or break a record. It involved hundreds of people in hundreds of ways, all doing their bit and all as important as the next man. In many ways, we were just the front men for an extraordinary group of people behind the scenes who got us to the start line. In return, I hoped our endeavour would continue to bring out that spirit in people and I wanted to do everything to make sure the magic got spread around.

The final morning before the boat was to leave for Canada was special. I had planned to be alone on board. It was very early on a grey, drizzly Monday morning when I drove down to Portsmouth and went to fetch the boat from the naval base. The sea was glassy calm, disturbed only by the steady rain. I glanced at my watch and saw I had some time to spare before I was due to arrive at Southampton docks, so I decided to make a slight detour, to the south and my childhood, and pointed the boat towards the Isle of Wight.

Everything was still and quiet when I arrived at Bembridge harbour, not a sound; but it had never been like this when I was a child. In the morning mist, all I could see was memories of jostling boats and dinghies, me and my friends messing around, our fathers frantically shouting from the beach, of fun and happiness, of bumps and bruises and laughter, above all of laughter. Right there I felt Dad standing quietly beside me.

The engine was scarcely idling as I chugged quietly around the harbour. And, as if from somewhere deep inside, I found tears were now running freely down my cheeks for the first time in ages.

I passed slowly by the pontoon at the Sailing Club. The members of this club had so much wanted to support this expedition; they were awash with friendship but not with funds. None the less, they organized a whip-round in the bar for the Prince's Trust, and I placed their sticker on the boat. That was the only logo placed on the boat for free. It was different. It was part of me.

As I left Bembridge harbour, I found myself waving nostalgically, not at anyone or anything in particular, just waving goodbye.

When I eventually reached Southampton, I tied up near

an enormous container ship alongside massive grey fenders that dwarfed our tiny boat. Everything suddenly felt very small. A huge crane swung over and plucked the boat out and on to a trailer. The tubes were deflated, and everything was neatly packed away before our precious cargo was steered through the vast gates in the bow, right into the guts of the ship.

Between us, we had designed and built what must have been one of the most advanced RIBs in the world. But beside this cavernous container ship it looked like a Dinky toy. As she disappeared from view, I felt that sense of sadness you experience when you reach the end of a long road.

There had been many days when the expedition seemed unlikely to get off the ground, but now we were here on the docks. The next time I would see her would be in a very different harbour, thousands of miles away and further north, on the remote Nova Scotia coastline. I was meant to be doing a BBC TV interview on the quayside but found it hard to make much sense. The container ship's gates closed. I glanced over my shoulder and our RIB was gone.

There wasn't much more we could now do. For the first time in months, the kit was ready and packed, the boat had gone, the logistics were in place as far as they could be, and the team's mood was high. The final countdown had started, and this stage can be frightening. Everything goes quiet and, maybe for the first time in ages, you have the opportunity to think about what really lies ahead.

I was beginning to understand a bit more now about what

we were undertaking. It was no longer happening 'next year'. It was almost upon us; and suddenly it felt so soon.

Shara had given birth to our son Jesse only four weeks earlier. It had been the most intense and intimate day of my life. He was perfect, and Shara, in those moments, had looked so alive. But in those first few weeks afterwards, I began to feel real doubts about everything ahead. I wasn't even sure why I was leaving at all, and when I sat and thought about it, I felt utterly torn.

It had been different with the Everest expedition. Then I was younger and maybe more rash, but Everest had changed me. When friends die in the mountains, you reconsider what those odds really mean. They are not just statistics any longer. They are real, and if you play them often enough you don't always come out on top.

Now my life was different. I was a husband and a father. I had much more to lose. I was no longer prepared to die up a mountain. Shara and Jesse had given me life after Dad passed on. I had everything to live for, and I wanted to stay alive. The idea of taking that level of risk again terrified me.

I didn't even know what the risks were here. No one did. So few people had tried to cross the North Atlantic in an open RIB that there were no stark statistics like the one in eight fatalities on Everest. There was nothing: no quantifiable ratio, no survival odds, just the unknown.

I tried to look for the positives. I tried to tell myself that my new family would make me more cautious, more determined to get home safely. But I wasn't sure that I believed it.

Only a matter of days before we were due to leave, I woke up in the middle of the night and knew I should a write a letter to Shara, just in case. I'd hand this letter to my best buddy, Charlie Mackesy, and ask him to give it to her only in one event – if I didn't come home. It was the hardest letter I have ever written. As I wrote, my palms clammy with sweat, the night seemed to stand still. I was confronting the worst option and trying to deal with the consequences. All the time I was praying – praying my wife would never have to read these words.

The last two years had been hard for Shara. And I owe her so much. It's obviously not ideal for any new mother that her husband should have to be away when their child is so small; and it's definitely not ideal that 'away' should mean setting off across a dangerous ocean in a small, open boat. Yet as the days neared we somehow never spoke of saying goodbye. It was our unwritten rule.

Charlie, Shaun White, the boat-builder, and I were due to fly from Heathrow to Nova Scotia on the Monday evening. Andy had already been there for three days, preparing the boat, while Mick and Nige were going to fly a day later. On the Friday evening, Shara gave me a little photograph album she had made, full of pictures of her and Jesse. It was beautiful.

Early the following morning I woke early and spoke for

the first time into the Dictaphone that would be my companion for so much of the time ahead.

It's 5 a.m., and I can't sleep. Shara is lying beside me, and Jesse is asleep on my pillow. I am trying to get packed up quietly, but I am so scared now. I am used to leaving for expeditions, but this is different – I feel strangely alone. Just looking at Shara and Jesse asleep is so hard. It breaks my heart.

I am so excited to be seeing those cold waters, but I am under no illusions that it's going to be anything but many weeks of being wet and frightened. But I still firmly believe it is possible. I just have to remind myself of that, and always remember that each wave is a wave closer back to my home.

As a team we had agreed to take $10,000 in cash, just in case we found ourselves in situations where perhaps a fisherman or a helicopter pilot, or anyone, needed some persuading. I wandered down to the bank and collected the money. It was a beautiful summer's day, and I was wearing just an old pair of shorts. I collected the money, and also bought a crate of Bell's whisky from the off-licence next door. With dollars and whisky, we now had international currency.

I played a last game of squash with Danny, the second-hand car dealer who plays a wily game with me several times a week. Afterwards he said, very gently, 'You know, Bear, I really don't want you to go.'

I just smiled back.

'Can't I just puncture the boat or something?' he asked.

In the afternoon we gathered everything Shara and Jesse needed to take to her mother's house and packed it into our car. We laughed. They were going down to the country with all seventeen suitcases. I was going across the North Atlantic, and I had two small bags.

Sunday drifted by. The sun shone, Charlie Mackesy came down, and we all lay on the grass and drank tea. I went for a walk with Shara and held her hand as I love to do. And then it was time to leave for the airport.

British Airways had generously provided our one-way tickets to Canada and they had kindly offered to show us around the weather centre at their headquarters at Heathrow before we left. As we approached their corporate head-quarters, I saw a welcoming party of BA staff, dressed in hats and uniforms. It was a lovely gesture on their part, but my mind was elsewhere. They were all watching.

I gave Jesse a little kiss, then turned to face Shara. She was crying already.

'Trust me, my love, all will be fine.'

I held her tight to try to stop the tears.

'We'll be safe and back together in no time. I promise.'

It was a promise I knew wasn't mine to make.

As we toured round BA's Compass House, I was in a daze. I couldn't take anything in. All I could think about was them both driving home, and Shara being so afraid. But I didn't know what else I could do. It was time to be a leader now, time to make sure we did this job properly, time to make sure I was right when I promised her we'd be OK. It was time to look ahead.

When we eventually reached the check-in area, I received

a text message from my sister Lara saying she hoped everything would go 'swimmingly'. It was quite funny.

My great-uncle Edward, aged ninety-three, called soon afterwards to wish me well. 'God bless you,' he said very slowly, and then he added in the softest and most tender of voices, 'We do so love you.'

What a gorgeous man he is.

I was feeling pretty drained, physically and emotionally, by the time Charlie and I settled into our seats. BA had put us in business class and we were soon being spoiled with champagne and food. Charlie was really buzzing, chatting to the crew about the expedition and generally enjoying every minute. He was in heaven. He eventually fell asleep snoring.

I just sat quietly, alone with my thoughts, staring out of the window. Now and then I could see the ocean, briefly visible between the clouds, and watch the white horses far below. I eventually closed my eyes as well, warm and snug, knowing that the way home would be a very different story.

5. NORTH FROM NOVA SCOTIA

A real friend is one who walks in when the rest of the world walks out.

Ronald Reagan

Even if all five of us had been born and bred in Halifax, Nova Scotia, it is hard to imagine how the people of this open-hearted Canadian city could have been more hospitable and supportive. The fact was that we were five British men who happened to have chosen their city as the starting point of our transatlantic expedition, and we had certainly not expected, nor did we deserve, the warm generosity shown to us by so many people.

Our boat, the *Arnold and Son Explorer*, was moored at the central quay in the middle of a waterfront development, and as soon as one of us stepped past the spectators to go aboard, we were asked for autographs and quizzed about the boat.

We were given free use of two nearby apartments for as long as we needed, and local officers of the Canadian navy gave us 3,000 litres of fuel, for which they refused to let us pay. Ordinary citizens of Halifax seemed drawn to the boat, coming to wish us well, offering us some piece of advice about the waters ahead. We were showered with kindness and all felt looked after and special.

Andy had already spent three days out here before us and seemed to have become something of a local celebrity through his press and television interviews. It was great to see. He was clearly enjoying himself and, just as I had hoped, he had really started to take ownership of his part of the expedition.

Amid the high spirits, though, there was plenty of work to be done to get the boat ready, and it soon became clear Andy had done a superb job in this respect as well. He had fitted a new alternator the day before we arrived, and it seemed to have solved a last-minute issue we had had with a faulty power supply. The boat was neatly stowed with most of the kit, apart from our personal stuff, and she looked fantastic. I felt so proud and very protective.

She had started out as a rough idea in our minds, advanced to the drawing board, been to the Boat Show, on to the sea trials, across the Atlantic in the huge container ship, and now here she stood in pride of place on the Halifax waterfront.

The food packages had been carefully sorted out into days, and Andy had been meticulous in making sure that everything was neat and tidy on board. That was important to me. Even before the building process was complete, I had gone out and bought more than 100 bungee elastic cords, and roll after roll of Gaffa sticky tape. Andy had laughed incessantly about this.

'I hope that crane is strong enough when she is lifted over the docks,' I said, as our pride and joy first went into the water in Portsmouth.

'Well, we could always bungee or Gaffa tape her together if it isn't,' Andy instantly replied.

Whatever we were doing on the boat, there was always a bungee near at hand. It became a running joke. In my experience, the army would grind to a halt if it wasn't for bungees and Gaffa tape. They are the meat and drink of any unit.

'We'll use 'em all,' I would always reply.

And I was right. By the end of the expedition, when we were finally packing up in Scotland, I took immense satisfaction from seeing Andy rummaging around in the hold of the boat, looking for a bungee to keep his holdall together, and then hearing him say, 'I don't believe it. We're out of bungees.'

Come Halifax, the stores were all lashed neatly down in place. Nothing could budge. The bungees were all working.

We knew we were going to be thrown around violently on the ocean, so everything needed to be really well secured. The flares, the food, the spares, everything – even down to the box of ear defenders that were never used. (This was because they made us sick, as they took away our instinctive balance.) The sea anchor was neatly folded and stowed ready for deployment and, all in all, our little yellow boat looked ready for anything. It was a fantastic sight.

I had brought with me around forty laminated stickers, featuring little motivational slogans, which I placed in strategic positions around the boat. All of the guys teased me incessantly about these. They told me they were quite unBritish, but I thought these sayings would help us get through when times were tough.

They served their purpose well, although I did concede that the sticker reading, 'Make sure you watch the sunset once a year – it will give you a whole new perspective on life' was starting to wear a little thin by the end. As Charlie wryly pointed out at the end of the 3,000 miles: 'Well, that's my sunsets done for the next twenty years.'

Our entire experience in Halifax was facilitated by the enthusiastic support of one of our lead sponsors, General Motors (Canada). I had made a speech at a GM conference in Italy some time before, and they had agreed to take one of the £15,000 sponsorship packages. They also effectively adopted this stage of the expedition, helping to generate publicity, raising money for a local charity – the Nova Scotia Sailing School, which teaches local kids how to build a boat and take trips into the wilderness (not round the Arctic if they've got any sense!) – and also hosting a farewell banquet for 500 people the night before we were to leave.

It was an emotional occasion. I had been asked to speak and accepted, even though I knew I would be speaking at about 3 a.m. British time, which I was still on, having arrived the day before.

The worst thing about speaking after dinner, though, is that it ruins your appetite. 'So much for taking this last chance to bulk up,' I thought, as I nervously played with my steak.

In fact I was too nervous to eat at all. It's weird how, after all the speeches I make – almost a hundred a year – I still get terrified. I dread those moments before you stand up, that silence as all eyes are on you, that intensity, but I guess to do it well you have to *use* that intensity. It's any speaker's best tool.

The first speaker was Michael Grimaldi, the president of General Motors (Canada), and he spoke concisely and directly about his company's pioneering spirit and how it constantly aimed to push back the boundaries in the automotive industry.

Then I stood up. All I really wanted to say was this: how so often people look at us and think that we are the pioneers and the guys breaking new boundaries, but it's not really true. In truth we are just normal guys who have been given a chance, a chance to follow a dream made possible by the likes of them. 'I'm not feeling very oratory-like right now,' I went on. 'I am nervous and we leave in only a few hours. But what I really want to say is thank you. It's because of your pioneering spirit that we are here. And when it comes down to those crunch times, somewhere out there in the waves and ice, the times when it really matters, I hope we can show that same spirit; and that we come home safe and can say, "We did you proud as well." Thank you.'

I sat down relieved, my job done. It was our last night, and I needed a bar and a strong drink.

As we left we said our thanks and farewells to the president of General Motors, and on the spur of the moment I offered him a quick spin on the boat the following day before we left.

'Unfortunately I am flying back to Toronto for a meeting tomorrow morning,' he said.

I paused, then asked again. 'How about doing it early?'

'That would be wonderful,' he smiled.

So at 6 a.m. the following day, in a crisp early-morning chill, under a clear Halifax sky, three of us took GM's president around the harbour. We were flying along over still, glassy seas at 25 knots. We watched the first of those sunrises, and it was a magical time.

Just before nine o'clock on that morning of Thursday, 31 July 2003, with barely an hour left before our scheduled departure, we were all sitting quietly around the boat, waiting. This was a rare period of calm and, in crisp sunshine, I decided it was the ideal time to convey a message. Standing on the bow, I asked Andy, Nige, Mick and Charlie for their attention. They turned to face me.

'Chloë has just faxed me a letter that was delivered to our base in London earlier this morning,' I said. 'I want to read it to you.' The letter was from the Prince of Wales.

Dear Bear,

I did just want to wish you and your team 'God Speed' for your intrepid adventure. I am delighted that the spirit of the Great British Eccentric Adventurer is alive and well and I much look forward to seeing you on your return.

Never has a Prince's Trust Ambassador gone to such lengths to support my Trust, and I am hugely grateful to you!

This comes with every possible thought and countless best wishes.

Yours most sincerely,

Charles

We were far from home, standing nervously on the brink of a life-changing challenge, and everybody was apprehensive. As messages of encouragement go, this handwritten letter from the Prince of Wales was hard to beat, and I could see it on the others' faces.

At last we were ready, and a flotilla of boats had gathered just off the quayside to escort us away from Halifax. There were 3,050 miles ahead of us. It was all systems go.

Almost.

It was 10 a.m., our time of departure, but there was no sign of Carol, the American journalist.

I had told her very firmly the previous evening that if she was late, we would leave without her.

She was late. So we were leaving.

'No, we can't go,' said Mick. 'You have to give her another ten minutes.'

'Five,' I replied.

The fleet of tugs, yachts and icebreakers was now moving out of the harbour, and people were glancing at their watches, wondering what was going on, what was causing the delay.

Quarter past ten, twenty past ten, half past ten. All our patience was being stretched. I could sense it. This wasn't what the guys needed. We were ready to go.

Carol McFadden was a beautiful, extremely glamorous and very game journalist from New York. The whole idea of taking her along for the first ten hours of the first leg of the expedition had started when she came to London and said she wanted to write an article about the world of expeditions for *Cosmopolitan.*

She was engaging, bright and entertaining, and, even though we were meeting at a time when the corporate rejection letters were arriving on a regular basis, I really enjoyed our conversation on the top deck of our barge.

'Well,' I said, 'if you want to get a real taste of the expedition, you should come with us for a bit of the first leg, from Halifax up the Nova Scotia coast.'

Carol's eyes literally flared into life, and she asked, 'Could I?'

'It would be a one-off and it would have a price,' I continued. 'Usually, press time is press time, expedition time is expedition time; we never mix it. But this would be an exception.'

'Well, that sounds a great idea,' she said.

'OK, this is the deal,' I said, thinking on my feet, intensely aware of what was then our very real need to raise funds. 'You can either write a normal article on the basis of our interview today or you could come along for part of the first leg, have the adventure of a lifetime and write a story about what it's *really* like to be on an expedition with five men on a small boat.'

I said it would have a price tag of £25,000.

Carol thought about it. It was a one-off opportunity. 'Inside an expedition' was a hundred times more saleable than just 'an expedition'. She agreed right there on the deck.

I knew we were offering a unique experience, and we were asking a premium price, but it was her call. On balance, I hoped it was a reasonable proposal.

Carol was a mother of four, leading a comfortable home life, but, there and then, she showed she was also gutsy, spontaneous and, above all, willing to grab life and have a go.

When I told Mick about the arrangement I had made with her, he congratulated me on what seemed a novel way of raising funds, but said we must make sure she signed some kind of indemnity.

'If anything happens to her, those Manhattan lawyers will sue you at the drop of a hat,' he warned.

'Well, will you write this indemnity form for me?' I asked him. 'Thanks, Miguel.'

Mick eventually produced a brief, very blunt document which, remarkably, managed to include the word 'death' eleven times in the space of only five lines.

'Mick, I can't send that to Carol,' I replied. 'She'll run a mile.' He told me just to send it. So I did. I think the wording surprised her but, again to her great credit, she signed on the dotted line the very same day.

She later told me, 'I sure wasn't going to let my husband see that. You Brits, you're nuts. You're meant to be looking after me, not sending through suicide notes to sign!'

Well, she'd passed Mick's litmus test.

We kept in regular touch during the preparations. At one stage, I arranged to take Carol over to Cowes for an afternoon on the boat. The aim was to give her all her kit and introduce her to what it was like on board. It was actually quite a blustery, overcast day, and I told her the sea could get pretty rough.

She didn't seem too concerned, but I glanced apprehensively at her equipment, which seemed to include, instead of a Musto offshore jacket, an Apple Mac i-pod, a silver-plated Theo Fennell pot of lip-balm and a Dolce and Gabbana headdress.

'Seriously, I would store some of that away,' I said.

'Baa,' she said, laughing.

It was one hell of an afternoon.

And sure enough, for the next month, we kept finding lip-gloss and Armani scrunchies wedged in between fuel filters or bilge alarms. Several times Andy appeared from the engine compartment staring at some beauty accessory in disbelief. It became a running joke.

Carol evidently lived in style and, true to form, she arrived in Halifax with her husband, the high-profile New York financier George McFadden, and their children. From the word go, they all joined in the spirit of the expedition. I remember one night in Halifax when Charlie leaned over to George, nudged him and told him to hurry up and drink his beer. He wanted to move on. No one usually talked to George like that and he loved it. It was a pleasure to have the McFaddens around.

The original plan was that Carol would remain on the

boat for the entire first leg but, when it emerged that there was no decent landing strip for her to be able to fly back from Port aux Basques, we modified the itinerary. Instead, we agreed we should take her up the coast for some ten hours, until late on the first night, then drop her off at a small inlet called Glace Bay, on the northernmost tip of Nova Scotia. There was a small airport there.

As arranged, she came down to the quay the day before we were due to leave, and I presented her with all her remaining equipment. With the kids standing by and clearly loving every minute, I gave their mum a big survival knife and harness, protective waterproof clothing, flares, torches, EPIRBs and the rest.

'OK, Carol,' I said finally. 'That's you set. You've got all your gear. Now, please make sure you are here at ten o'clock in the morning. We will leave at ten prompt.'

Those were the famous last words. It was now 10.35 and there was still no sign of Carol.

Finally, in a frenzied flurry of bags and taxis, she arrived at 10.40, forty minutes late.

'I'm so sorry,' she said as she kissed her family goodbye and clambered aboard.

'Come on, Carol,' I said. 'We'll talk about this later.'

I subsequently learned Carol was late because she was on the telephone to poor Chloë in London checking on all our insurance policies for her. I had taken personal cover for all the crew while we were in Canadian waters and included her on the policy.

'Well, if you hadn't got me so worried with that death warrant you sent me . . .' she explained, and as she spoke I saw Mick fumbling with the rope he was stowing.

I smiled and kind of understood. She was aboard, and she was fine, and we were finally on our way.

So, with the nose of our boat pointing north, we edged away from Halifax, escorted by this wonderful flotilla of local boats. We waved at them, and they waved at us, and I found my heart was pounding. So many people in this town had done so much for so little reward. We'd miss them, but we had a job to do now.

As we left the city behind us, I felt a peace, a quietness. It was such a relief after so long to just be us. Alone. No mass of people, no more interviews, no more anything apart from what we could bring to this ourselves. We were as well equipped and trained as we could be and we all felt proud to be here. The sea was mirror calm, the sky clear, and I sat on my own with my feet over the prow. I closed my eyes and breathed in the cold Nova Scotia air. The hull, with all those signatures from the Boat Show now painted over, glided though the water with ease, and I found myself thinking of Shara all those miles away, safe at home.

Carol settled as we picked up speed, and I quietly sat back and thanked God that we had a calm day and a flat sea. She was not short on courage, but I am not sure whether she would have coped very well if conditions had been really rough.

Several days later, when the boat was being thrown around and we were all being repeatedly drenched by sprays of icy water, Charlie suddenly piped up from deep within his survival suit pulled over his head: 'I think Carol would be looking for an exit strategy by now, don't you reckon?'

I think that was a fair response. But to her credit she had agreed to come whatever the weather, more or less.

Mick obviously gave the whole subject some thought and, some weeks later, over a beer in Iceland, he turned quite serious and said, 'Do you know, if we had been caught in a storm when Carol was on board, I think we would have had no option.'

'To do what?'

Carefully measuring his words, he replied, 'In those sort of horrendous conditions, not just with Carol but with anyone who was unprepared for that kind of onslaught, I think you would have had no choice but to tie their arms and legs together and strap them down in the sardine tin until we were out of trouble.

'She wouldn't have liked it,' he added between sips, 'but at least she would have survived.'

We all looked at Mick, a little concerned.

Mercifully, the conditions did not arise where Mick had the opportunity to test his theory on Carol. A gentle breeze ensured her day unfolded with no greater alarm than our first sighting of a minke whale.

Into the afternoon, we gave her a chance to helm. I told her it was her watch, and she should take the wheel. She seemed uncertain whether I was serious but, in exactly the manner we had grown to expect, and actually respect, she just got up and took over.

I gave her the bearings and showed her the direction we needed to take. She stared intently ahead, but we were soon doing figures of eight in the ocean. Anybody watching our path from above would have assumed we were trying to signal SOS in the water, but Mick stepped forward as Carol's personal tutor.

'OK, now this is going to be easy,' he began. 'Just imagine ... you are driving this boat down Fifth Avenue in Manhattan. Prada is over on your right, Dolce and Gabbana is on your left. Go straight ahead up Fifth, aiming straight towards Gucci on the horizon.'

Her course became as straight as an arrow.

She was laughing, and was always a good sport. Despite all the endless jokes, each of us was highly impressed by the fact that someone like her had risen to the challenge, done everything expected and walked the walk. For all she knew, it could have been blowing a Force Eight gale out there. And as for the banter, well, that just meant everyone had accepted her.

We arrived at Glace Bay just before midnight, still in calm seas. The sun had long since disappeared in a distant glow of orange across the sky and we had all sat mesmerized, lost in our own thoughts. I felt so calm and content.

Nige had navigated us carefully through the myriad of tiny islets around the bay itself, and it was strange to pass by so many moss-covered rocks, sometimes just 30 yards away. Nige was concentrating intently on the GPS screen.

'Left five degrees, and hold the course for 300 metres,' he would say quietly. He was in his element, using the precision accuracy of the Simrad navigational equipment to chart a safe course and ensure we avoided those lethal outcrops.

Finally, we entered the tiny harbour itself, and noticed more than a hundred little fishing boats moored together in a small bay. The fishermen were working in silence by halogen light, processing their catch, and the whole place was dominated by an overpowering stench of fish innards. As we glided silently up the narrowing creek, the locals seemed to hardly notice us.

We moored and found that the only place open around the dock was the small ambulance station, with its doors open, so we went in there. The crew on the nightshift seemed surprised to see five massively overdressed men shuffle into their hangar, and they were intrigued to hear what we were doing. They could not have been more friendly, and they generously plied us with sandwiches and cups of hot tea.

It was soon time for us to say our goodbyes to Carol, and we found her a taxi that would take her on to the hotel she was staying at, near the airport, from where she would fly home.

'Thank you all so much,' she said. 'It's been amazing. It's been a real privilege to have shared these early moments with you. I will think of you all every moment until you are home safe. Look after each other, eh?'

'We will,' we promised.

Soon after 1 a.m., we were heading on out again towards Port aux Basques, a small town on the southern tip of Newfoundland, the huge island that sits to the north of Nova Scotia. Once again we wove a careful path through the small islands and rocks, each still beautifully silhouetted in the moonlight, until finally we were in open water.

It was 100 miles straight across this stretch of water to Port aux Basques, where we planned to refuel before heading up to our final Canadian port on the tip end of the Labrador coast, far to the north.

At about 3 a.m. Charlie was on watch and his attention was drawn by a green glow in the sky to the north.

'What's that?'

'It must be the lights of Newfoundland,' Nige suggested.

But Newfoundland is a huge, magnificent wilderness, not a city electrified and lit for 10 million inhabitants.

'Or maybe it's an oil rig,' I wondered.

'No way,' Andy replied. 'That's the northern lights.'

And it was. This was nature's famous lightshow, staged every night at the northern end of the planet. We sat in wonder. The effect was stunning, as if the sky was being illuminated by the stage-lights of some sort of heavenly concert. We sat entranced, in the world's biggest and most spectacular arena.

Our expectation after that first night was that we would be treated to this natural extravaganza most nights across the freezing ocean ahead. However, we never saw them again.

The weather made sure of that. More often than not, dense cloud cover obscured the northern lights and gave us long, dark nights.

But that was all in the future. For now, on this first night of the expedition, the five of us settled back, enjoyed the view and picked contentedly at our boil-in-the-bag sachets of baked beans. That night, it was impossible not to feel richly blessed.

The northern lights lasted until around 4 a.m., and Mick and I helmed through that last night-time shift before dawn, while the others snatched a couple of hours' rest in the sardine tin. In a tranquil, misty dawn we pulled into Port aux Basques at just after 6.30 a.m.

We could hardly have been luckier with the way things were going so far. Everyone was slipping into their role and feeling confident. Each of us was playing our part with one clear goal in mind: to stay alive and complete the crossing. If it was going to be like this every day and night, then it would be easy. Privately, we knew that wouldn't happen. It was only ever a matter of time before the skies and seas would change.

As we approached the quay at Port aux Basques, I spotted the harbourmaster standing by to welcome us. He had been telephoned and forewarned by Chloë. The tracker system had kept her informed of our every move, and her attention to small details like this had an enormous impact on the expedition. It was the difference between being warmly greeted on arrival at a far-flung outpost and arriving and trying to find someone to talk to and having to explain who we were.

'Welcome to Port aux Basques,' declared the harbour-master with a broad smile.

I had expected this place to be a major hub for shipping in the area. It was, after all, one of the last 'big' ports before the northern waters of the Arctic ahead and a staging post for shipping between Newfoundland and mainland Canada. Instead, there were just a few old concrete and wooden piers stretching out to sea, where the big icebreakers and ferries could refuel and disembark.

The rapidly rising sun was warming the cold air of dawn, and, happy to have arrived, we all began to peel off the layers of dry suits, thermals, Gortex and waterproofs.

A group of local fishermen were sitting on the wooden walkway at the head of our pier. Leaning over the railings, side by side, smoking silently, they were dressed in lumber-jack shirts and chest-high rough waterproofs and were watching us cautiously as we bustled about the boat.

I was now down to my undies, and felt deeply relieved to have got rid of all the heavy, stinking kit, which now lay in a pile on the foredeck. Right then, I realized we needed some more rope and, on the foreshore, I happened to spot an old corrugated building with a sign marked 'supplies'.

They would have what we needed, but I really didn't fancy getting dressed in all my kit again. I glanced over at the fishermen and thought, well, I am sure they have seen a man in his underwear before. So I pulled on my Musto ocean boots, took a deep breath and, dressed in nothing apart from underpants and boots, walked gingerly past the fishermen to the shop.

They looked at me, looked at each other, then stared out to sea, puffing on their cigarettes, without saying a word. Charlie, chortling, caught the whole scene on camera.

The sun was shining on a clear morning, and I was wandering around a chandlery in my pants. I was in heaven.

6. SURFING THE WAVES

Man cannot discover new oceans unless he first loses sight of the shore.

Christopher Columbus

British people traditionally seem fascinated by trying to forecast the weather. It's a national obsession: we watch the news and then we watch the weather. It never serves much purpose, save the vague satisfaction, upon hearing the rain on the roof, of noting whether or not the forecasters were correct. This is a strange pastime, and one at which my mother-in-law is a maestro.

'Hmm,' Vinnie often muses from her sofa when it starts to pour outside, 'they were right.'

She assumes this is, of course, highly irregular.

Out on the North Atlantic, though, the stakes were a bit higher than whether or not it would drizzle during the summer fête.

For us, the weather forecast was everything. If our expedition was going to go smoothly, it would probably be because we got the weather forecast right. Similarly, if the expedition ended in disaster, it was more than likely going to be because our weather forecast was wrong. This worried me. So much seemed to hang on these forecasts . . . our lives in particular; and so many of those forecasts, ultimately, appeared to be down to luck.

We were not looking for rough seas and storms – there

was too much at stake. We didn't want to be heroes – all we wanted was to be safe. We would stay safe by getting the forecast right.

It was as simple as that.

Everything I wanted most in the world – to get back safely to Shara and Jesse, to be the best husband and the best dad I could be – depended on accurate weather forecasting and staying away from the bad stuff.

Plenty of other factors could go wrong, but the implications of bad weather were by far the greatest danger. In such an exposed, small boat, we were highly vulnerable.

Andy, with his experience of the sea, was well aware of our precarious circumstances. In March, some months before we set off, he was on board HMS *Newcastle* in heavy seas off the coast of Cornwall. HMS *Newcastle* is a type-42 Destroyer, 462 feet in length, and, from his position on the bridge, with hundreds of tonnes of wild water pouring over her bows, the ship pitching wildly as she battled through the blackness, Andy began to understand how vulnerable we would be in an open RIB, only 33 feet long. He knew as well as we all did that the forecasting really mattered.

As soon as we arrived in Port aux Basques, I took time with Mick to check the weather forecast. This would become a ritual: whenever we arrived in port, Mick and I would use our first spare moments to research the weather and call Mike Town in the UK.

Mike is one of the top meteorologists in Britain and was

one of the few experts to predict the hurricane in 1987. We were extremely lucky to have him on hand.

We got through to him on the satellite (SAT) phone first time.

It was our first call back from the boat. Our system of hunting good weather had begun. It was midday back in England, and this was just about the only occasion when Mike Town would be called at a sensible time of day. Unfortunately, we ended up calling him at all times of the nights ahead, but he was kind enough to expect and accept these calls whenever they came. He understood only too well how much we relied on him.

'We're in Port aux Basques. How does the weather look from here?'

'It's looking OK,' he replied. 'You shouldn't have any problems for the next twenty-four hours.'

'So it's clear?' Mick asked.

'Pretty much. There are a few localized small fronts but nothing really menacing. There's a big storm passing to your south, but that should miss you. The temperature will drop from here onwards, but you shouldn't find more than Force Five northerlies, and they're going your way. It should be fine.'

When I first met Mike I called him 'sir'. He was my geography teacher at school, but he soon became a friend as well. He was a climber and a martial artist and a real character, loved by many of his students. He used to arrange climbing trips to the Lake District, which Mick and I, aged fifteen, adored and took very seriously. For both of us, he became genuinely inspirational, and we have stayed in touch with him ever since leaving school.

Soon after meeting Shara, I planned to take her away for a weekend's climbing. Shara was under the impression it was purely a romantic getaway weekend, which it was of sorts, but it did also involve two ascents of Skiddaw, the hard way. It was Mike who lent me the keys to his cottage in Cumbria.

In the years when I was training with the army, Mike used to pack stones in my rucksack and run off ahead up the mountains, dragged by two abnormally large Bernese mountain dogs, telling me to hurry up because he had the sandwiches.

Time and again, Mike has been a source of support and friendship, a man I have learned to trust absolutely. And I loved the fact that he had been one of the few to predict the hurricane!

Some people might think it is a bit unusual, maybe a bit amateurish, to set out across the North Atlantic with your old geography teacher as one of your main sources of meteorological advice. But I liked that. I suppose I was just lucky that my old geography teacher happened to be such an expert in this field.

The Fleet Weather Centre, operated by the navy, also provided us with invaluable information at various stages of the expedition, and when Internet access was available in port we logged on to various weather websites, including one maintained by, and designed for, the US military.

Our third source of guidance was the local population. The people living in these isolated and far-flung places were not slow to offer their opinions on the weather. Down the years, through the generations, they had learned to interpret and recognize patterns; to look at the sky, feel the wind and trust their instincts.

The bottom line was that we were trying to avoid the storms, and these people were fishermen by trade. Avoiding the storms was what they had to do every day of every year of their lives.

In Port aux Basques, the local people seemed relaxed about the weather. Wizened old men appeared near the dock later in the morning and told us how they had only just emerged from nineteen days of dense fog, but now things seemed to be clearing.

'You should still be careful,' said one old man, dressed in a thick woollen jersey and faded jeans. 'Things can change very quickly out there.'

Routinely, we were used to predicting the weather for a journey of, say, 60 miles offshore. That is still a long way out to sea. But we needed now to estimate the conditions for a crossing as long as almost 1,000 miles. That was a whole different beast.

You might be told that wind speed was only 5 to 10 knots, and think that is all right, but a wind just 20 per cent over that can still produce enormous swells. This in turn reduces the speed of the boat, and suddenly your carefully planned two-day forecast would have to become a three- or four-day guestimate ... and it was that extra time that was so unknown and dangerous.

We had always known that accurate forecasting would be difficult, not least because we would be passing through waters that were, to a large extent, uncharted. Where little shipping traffic passes, the authorities understandably don't place too many weather buoys, so information was sketchy and forecasts often unreliable.

Most of the time, we simply had to be satisfied with an accurate twenty-four-hour forecast, and thereafter we would make a reasonable assessment and hope. Above all, we simply tried to be cautious and sensible.

It was just before ten o'clock on another brisk and clear morning when the *Arnold and Son Explorer* pulled away from Port aux Basques. We had refuelled, paying for the diesel with a heavy fistful of our US$50 bills, taken from a watertight container in the depths of the hold where we stored our cash, passports, wallets and photographs of home. We said goodbye to the locals and once again pointed our nose north.

Within fifteen minutes, though, we were in dense sea fog, and we found ourselves edging through what felt like thick, soggy soup. The fog was so intense that at times it was impossible to see the bow of the boat. We were driving blind.

We had been warned of magnetic variables in this region, and the compass started to behave erratically. This was worrying. We were now relying entirely on the accuracy of our electrical instruments to make any progress at all.

Every now and then, through the mist, we caught a

glimpse of Newfoundland away to our right, a craggy stretch of coast or a distant lighthouse; then everything would go grey and damp again, enveloping us in mist. Everything gets wet in seconds as this type of fog hits you. Inexorably and quietly, it covers you in moisture.

The sea though stayed calm and flat, and we moved steadily on through this strange, silent seascape. Minute by minute, we were beginning to settle into a routine.

As the afternoon drew on, the temperature began to drop and the waves started to build steadily into a swell. The change was slow and gradual, but we were clearly approaching much bigger seas. We knew we were heading up towards the Belle Isle Strait, a natural funnel of water where the wind and currents drive the ice down between Newfoundland and Labrador. It was an infamous stretch of water, and not much used. It was dangerous and unpredictable and was now less than 300 miles to the north. We were readying ourselves.

Perceptibly, the feel of everything was changing. We were alone and heading north. It was only going to get colder and more isolated from now on and ice was ahead, somewhere. We had no idea how long it would be until we saw it, but it was out there, waiting, floating massively to our north. We knew that Port aux Basques was to be our last port of accessible civilization for a long time.

We were starting to quieten into our own worlds, checking and rechecking, lashing ourselves to the boat when we moved around, taking nothing for granted, keeping our own personal grab bags clipped to our waists. These small waterproof holdalls contained essential items such as a torch, a knife, a hand-held VHF radio and mini-flares.

Each of us was well stocked with anti-sickness pills, and these were working well. I took my pills on the dot every eight hours. I had to keep alert and avoid that debilitating sense of feeling wretched and disoriented.

The seasickness, we soon discovered, was often worst in the sardine tin, and if it hit you, it was utterly incapacitating. You lie there, desperately needing some decent rest, over-whelmed by the invasive smell of diesel and the deafening roar of the engine, and you are wet and cold. You can taste the salt water in your mouth and your nostrils are sore and raw, and your stomach churns, and nothing can stop it. You want nothing more than to curl up and die.

They say seasickness has two stages: one is when you don't care if you die; the second is when you start praying to die.

Whenever anybody was sick over the side, it was vital to try to rehydrate afterwards. You'd have to pump water from the large jerry cans strapped to the side of the console and start drinking again. It was the last thing you felt like doing, but it was absolutely necessary to recover your strength.

'Drink water. Replace the liquids. Keep drinking.' This became one of our mantras. Experience had told us that dehydration could be a big issue in an open boat, especially when it is rough. The sheer amount of waves and spray that was eventually to come over us meant that we swallowed a lot of salt water – it was impossible to avoid. This means your salt intake becomes very high and you need twice the amount of fresh water to compensate. But on the sea you never feel like drinking, which is why it has to be a discipline.

As we progressed, the rota seemed to be settling down and working well. We had decided to sustain a five-hour rota. Each crew member would helm for an hour, navigate for an hour, spend the next hour sitting in the 'deckchair', a piece of rubber material on one side, slung between two metal struts and angled down, and lastly rest in the sardine tin for two hours. Every hour on the hour, almost without exception, the five of us rotated religiously through this circuit of tasks and responsibilities.

Our concept was logical and straightforward: make the big challenges manageable by breaking them into smaller tasks. We reckoned that on a 1,000-mile leg you had to have something short-term to focus on. The days and hours passed very slowly sometimes, especially if you were sick. It was much easier to focus on getting through a single hour and then addressing a new situation than it was to have nothing to think about apart from watching the GPS plotter and seeing how slowly we were moving.

We humans are creatures of habit and we need something to focus on. This routine was something tangible that would hold us together when it struck rough, and I was determined that whatever happened, we would stick to it. Even when you were resting in the sardine tin, after one hour you would roll over to the other side as the guy to your right got up, and another body crawled in to your left.

There were times in those early days when we would be coasting along in calm seas under clear skies and one of us would suggest we stayed as we were because everyone was OK, but I was adamant we stuck to the rota.

This was our discipline. In extreme environments people depend on routines, and the more familiar you are with the routine, the less frightening the unfamiliar becomes. On the ocean, life gets much easier when you have something you can hold on to, something you know is predictable and reliable and constant. Whatever else might change, I wanted the rota to remain on track.

The only drawback of the system was that you had to get on well with whoever was next to you. The rota meant you really only had regular contact with the people either side of you. When the seas were rough, you would be wearing your helmet and full survival suit, and, even though you were sharing a living space of a few square yards, you would scarcely be aware of the other two members of the crew one seat away from you. It sounds strange, but at various stages of the expedition twenty-four hours would pass during which I would not see Andy even though we were never more than a yard apart.

Mick just loved this. He would say that this was his ideal holiday: no chit-chat, no small-talk, just the roar of the engine. He announced that if the rota format could be duplicated in England, life would definitely be better. This is a sure sign that a man is working too hard and getting too many phone calls.

Growing used to our equipment, and settling into the

hourly routine, we continued to make good progress, at times reaching speeds of 25 knots as the following seas propelled the boat forward.

I remembered how Andy had told me one evening that one of the reasons why he was so keen to do this expedition was his desire to experience some unusual sea conditions and, towards evening on this first day out of Port aux Basques, it was beginning to happen. We were being treated to the spectacular sensation of 'surfing' on big ocean breakers.

We had been aware of the sea building in size and strength throughout the day. Increasingly powerful waves would roll up from behind and raise the boat high above the ocean; then the crest of the wave would break, and we would surge forward. It was amazing. We would look back to see the wave frothing away in white water and, within moments, another surge of marine power would lift us high once again.

Roller followed roller, surge followed surge.

By dusk, the dense fog was returning, but we were still surfing forward at good speeds, more than ever trusting in our instruments to keep us on course. I started to wonder what would happen if while racing down one of these rollers we were propelled into a collision with an iceberg. At these speeds, and in the dark, we would have no time to react with the energy of the waves behind us. It was not a good thought, but I consoled myself by remembering being told that at this time of year we would not hit ice until much further north. We had to trust that and keep the speed on through the fog.

It had been a strange kind of day.

First the fog, then the falling temperatures, then the slowly swelling waves, then the darkness, finally all of this together. Piece by piece, element by element, the ocean seemed to be assembling its forces against us. Individually, none of these factors would have been a concern but, as they all massed together that first night, each of us had the distinct feeling that we were entering a new phase of the expedition. We were beginning the work in earnest. The playtime was over and we were entering the arena where mistakes would become extremely costly.

Each mile travelled to the north felt like a mile travelled to a different level. It was exciting, it was what we had put so much time and energy into preparing for, but I would be lying if I did not admit that my heart was beginning to pound.

The distant flash of a lighthouse through the mist and darkness reminded us how close we were to the coast, as the Belle Isle Strait narrowed towards its most northerly gap. The boat really needed to be driven now. Concentrate. Control her. Compensate for the power of the waves pulling you off course. Feel her.

The RIB was built for these conditions and she was thriving in the surf and this was what we had trained for. This was why we were here. There was nobody else around: just the waves, the fog, the boat and the five of us. This was living; these were the moments when I felt most alive.

As we approached the Strait, now only 50 miles to the north, I found myself privately trying to work out how the rota would unfold; who would be helming at the critical hour, guiding us through the currents and funnel of sea and racing tidal water. It would be me or Mick; I knew Mick would be thinking the same.

It was going to be difficult. There were no stars out, and in the fog it would be easy to lose all sense of direction and perspective.

At around midnight, when Charlie was at the helm, we found ourselves travelling in completely the wrong direction before he made a 180-degree turn and set us back on course. He cursed himself out loud, but it was so easy to do. The horizon and sea become a confused blend of rolling blackness. The chart-plotter screen is an eye-aching blur of green and reds. Tiredness pounds at your eyelids. The waves yank you violently off course and every small over-correction is replicated by the jet drive at the stern. The boat is so sensitive to helm.

Just before 1 a.m., I came off watch and Mick took over. It would be he who would helm us through the Belle Isle Strait ahead. He needed his concentration now and we all knew it. None of us slept and we all sat up and watched him guide us through, struggling to keep us on course in the roar of the surf behind.

It felt as if we were riding some kind of wild beast, all the time knowing that we could never be completely in control of something so powerful and untameable. As we surged forward, I found myself praying again that there would be no ice.

Again and again the boat rose and fell, as huge waves

lifted her hull before throwing us down the face of the wave in front.

Both time and sea were now racing.

An hour later, I was crouching down in the pitch black beside the console with my torch, trying to check one of the fuel gauges, when the boat was hit violently by a wave side-on. My head smashed against the metal console and I slumped back into the seat holding my forehead in my hands.

I shouted out loud, my eyes closed tight. I was feeling dazed and soon I had a splitting headache.

Charlie asked, 'Are you OK?'

'Yes, I'm fine,' I replied, wincing. 'Can you hold the torch while I just recheck this fuel gauge.'

This was always a tricky task; the fuel was stored in four areas and, for reasons relating to the distribution of weight and maximizing the boat's performance, we needed to drain the fuel from the centre tank first, then from the tanks on the side and lastly from the bladder at the front.

The whole system operated on a complex series of fuel drain levers and manifolds. Andy had marked them all for us to be able to read and understand, even at night.

I was on my knees trying to check the dial of the centre tank we were using, just to make sure it wasn't time to change over. This check involved pumping air into the tank and giving the dial time to settle before taking the reading.

'It looks fine,' I shouted to Charlie who was right next to me. 'The reading looks OK.'

The engine typically ticks over at 2,600 revs per minute,

producing a roar that would seem invasive for a short period but which, for us on the ocean, became almost hypnotically comforting after a while. That roar represented raw power and movement in the right direction, homewards. We grew to love it.

Fifteen minutes later, for no apparent reason, the noise began to die. The revs plummeted. Then it stopped. All of a sudden, our loud mechanical world plunged into a terrifying silence. From 450 hp to nothing, the boat was now running on momentum. The engine was dead.

Our hearts stopped.

It was approaching 2.30 a.m., and we were still in the last port of the Strait. Everyone was immediately awake and alert, fired with adrenalin, desperately trying to work out what needed to be done. Andy had been in the sardine tin, but he was out on his feet in a second, checking the levers, the filters, the engine monitoring systems, all lightning fast, instinctively moving into reaction mode.

'Get the engine lid up now,' he said calmly and firmly.

The rest of us reached for the latches and lifted the lid, as our naval engineer set about his work.

'She's out of fuel,' he said, his face contorting with strain as he grappled with the engine primer. 'We need to act fast. The turbo is not going to like this at all.'

He started frantically pumping the engine primer; pumping then priming. I stood over him, acutely aware that we were drifting powerlessly in one of the world's most treacherous stretches of water, vulnerable to any rogue wave.

Without the roar of the engine, for the first time we could hear the wind licking violently off the waves. It was much stronger, much more threatening than I had realized.

The sea was churning white and black, and suddenly we were just a little boat at the mercy of the sea. With no propulsion from the engine, we would have no ability to respond if one of these rollers hit us side-on. In the darkness, in what was the first major crisis of the expedition, I just hoped and prayed that Andy could get her working again.

Time seemed to be suspended.

We waited and waited.

Two and a half minutes passed like hours.

Then Andy looked at me, then back at the engine, and said loudly, 'Try her now.'

I took a breath and turned the key in the ignition.

There was a bubbling noise, a spluttering.

Then nothing.

'Again, Bear,' he said. 'And hold it.'

I did.

A deeper noise, and then a different noise, and then finally that comforting roar as the engine sprang into life and the boat came alive again.

Several hours later, Mick told me how his legs had turned to jelly when he heard that silence descend. Mine had too, and they stayed that way for several hours afterwards.

'Well done, buddy,' I said to Andy. 'Good work.'

'The central tank was empty. But I don't know how. Who last checked it?'

Central tank? Empty?

I knew what they meant.

'It was me,' I told everyone over the roar of the engine. 'I'm so sorry. I must have misread it. It won't happen again, I promise.'

We carried on in silence.

I knew I had caused the crisis. I had checked that tank just a few moments before and I must have misread the dial. Hitting my head was no excuse. I was angry with myself. It could have been disastrous. How could I have been so stupid, so careless?

With hindsight, it might have been a good thing that it was me who made the first mistake of the expedition. It was inevitable that there were going to be mistakes – it was only natural – but nobody wanted to be the first.

Maybe the fact that it was me, as leader, who had made the first cock-up took the pressure off the others, but I felt I had let them down a little. I remember my late father saying that if you want a good team, then pick people who are better than you. Most people do the opposite. It makes them feel better. But I had picked people who were better than me.

It was always our great strength.

It was with huge relief that we eventually turned and watched the Belle Isle Strait fade into the darkness behind.

The rest of the night wore on and just before dawn the mist lifted to reveal the black outline of the Labrador coast away to our left. The wind was biting and dramatically colder now, but we knew we had survived our first test.

'Wow, look at that!' Mick shouted suddenly.

I turned around to see an iceberg, which must have been the size of Buckingham Palace, half a mile away on the port side. It was incredible: huge, cold and grey. The waves rolled past it furiously.

We stared in disbelief. If we had collided with that during the night, there would only have been one survivor, and it would not have been us. Thank God, the fog was clearing.

'This is too early to be seeing ice,' I thought to myself. We had been told we wouldn't see ice until we were off the coast of Greenland. Seeing icebergs this far south was not a good sign. But I knew what I was seeing here off the port side. What worried me most though was what else we had been told that was wrong.

We had read that what you see of an iceberg represents no more than 6 per cent of its total mass; based on that fact, this berg was enormous. It seemed to belong here. In our small, yellow-tubed boat, I felt we didn't. We were trespassing, and we were alone. I felt as though the iceberg was looking at us, angry to be disturbed in its territory.

Some experts had warned us that icebergs might not show up on our radar screens, but this wasn't generally the case. In fact, the Canadian coastguards place radar reflectors on the large ones, and this gave us some reassurance – though not much.

The following seas continued to drive us on towards our destination, and we reckoned we would reach St Mary's harbour, on the Labrador coast, at around 6.30 a.m., approximately three hours ahead of schedule.

Andy was due to helm at five o'clock but he had just got off to sleep and, as a small gesture of apology for getting him up in the middle of the night when the engine stopped, I suggested I would do some of his shift. We were all tired.

By dawn, and only three miles from shore, we suddenly felt a rush of warm air on our faces. It was a welcome change from the cold winds that had been blowing all night, and with this wind came a rich aroma of heather. Labrador looked and smelled like the wilds of Scotland and, as we carefully wound our way from Battle Harbour down the mouth of the remote estuary to the port of St Mary's, all five of us were buzzing.

The land on either side of this narrow inlet was barren and untamed, but eventually we turned a corner and found a small harbour full of fishing boats, surrounded by a cluster of corrugated-iron buildings. It was early morning, but people were already at work on the one concrete quay, preparing thousands of freshly caught crabs.

Our early arrival had caught the local reception party by surprise, and we pulled alongside an old wooden pier to wait. We began to unwind and enjoy the quiet of the moment as we waited for the local contact to arrive and guide us to where we were to moor. We were so pleased to be here, safe and with some time to prepare for the first of our real tests ahead: the Labrador Sea.

We dug out the bottle of Mumm champagne we had brought to mark our first sighting of an iceberg and removed it from its bubble wrap. The cork flew off and the five of us drank contentedly.

However, within minutes, we were being bitten to shreds by giant mosquitoes and blood was pouring down Charlie's neck.

'Get the cigarettes out, quick,' he shouted, slapping his forehead frantically. 'That'll keep them away.'

It didn't.

Before long, each of us was covered in huge bites that oozed blood. They itched like hell. None of us had seen mosquitoes this big, and Nige said they obviously had to be this huge to survive so far north – they would need to be well insulated. Well, after such a feast of English blood, they would certainly be that all right.

As we scurried around, each clutching four cigarettes in both hands in a vain attempt to dispel the insects, we heard a voice behind us.

'Welcome! We weren't expecting you until half past nine.' The booming voice belonged to Alton Rumbolt, mayor of St Mary's.

'How do you do?' I replied, putting out my hand. 'Yes, we had following seas, and we've made good time.'

'OK, well, as soon as you are all sorted out, I will show you to where you are staying.'

Alton led us along a dirt track up the hill towards the harbour buildings, and almost everybody stopped to greet us as we walked by. They all seemed to know what we were doing, and they all seemed eager to help.

'Enjoy your stay in St Mary's,' said one of the fishermen.

'Thanks,' Nige replied.

We walked on.

Alton Rumbolt noted, 'That was Robert Rumbolt.'

'I see,' Nige said innocently. 'Is he your brother?'

'No . . . just a relative.'

It soon became clear that the majority of the population of St Mary's, which did not exceed 250 in total, was also named Rumbolt. And when it came to naming shops or businesses, it seemed they didn't like to venture too far from the path of convention: 'Rumbolt General Stores'; 'Rumbolt Fishing'; 'Rumbolt Supplies'.

Nige persevered: 'Is that your shop over there, Alton?'

'Nope,' Alton replied, 'that's my cousin's.'

'What about Rumbolt Repairs?'

By this stage, Nige was finding everything quite amusing. He had, after all, been at sea for a while.

'Not mine,' Alton replied. 'That's my second cousin's.'

We reached our rooms and crashed. Everyone was drained. Nobody had got much sleep in the sardine tin during the past two nights. It's not easy to fall asleep beside a roaring engine, bracing yourself every time a wave hits the boat. Sleep only tends to come when you are so exhausted that you physically can't stay awake. As Andy would tell people when asked how we slept, 'You can sleep anywhere if you're tired enough.'

In due course, Mick and I headed back down to the boat. We clambered inside the cubby, where Andy's spares and our supplies were stowed during passage, and dialled home on the SAT phone. We needed to speak first to Chloë, to update her on our progress, and then to Mike Town for an updated forecast.

More than ever, we were determined to get this next judgement exactly right. The next leg, across the infamous Labrador Sea to Greenland, would be one of the toughest of the entire expedition, and we didn't want to take any unnecessary risks. The passage through the Belle Isle Strait had been rougher than we'd expected and that had taught us a vital lesson. The forecast might say the outlook is fine, but the reality for a small boat in unpredictable seas can be very different. We weren't a big cruise liner or a frigate. We were effectively a rugged, inshore speedboat, and as far as forecasts were concerned, this was worth remembering.

Mike Town was not overly optimistic about the prospects.

'There's a north-westerly wind of around Force Four to Five,' he said, 'and you'll be heading north-east, so that will probably give you a beam sea for the crossing.'

'That's not ideal but it's manageable,' I said.

We checked a couple of websites, and they confirmed the likely direction of the wind. The data all forecast north-westerlies, and, for us, that meant beam seas.

Our kind of boat was most vulnerable in a beam sea. With the waves rolling across us, we have little lateral stability compared with either a head-on or following sea. I didn't like this.

Mike added cautiously, 'It looks as if the winds are going to get stronger, not weaker, after about forty-eight hours. But if you do decide to wait, you could be in St Mary's for a while.'

It made the decision much more difficult. Did we sit and wait, or risk it, getting most of the 700-mile crossing completed before the bad weather really kicked in?

I discussed this with Mick. He agreed we didn't want to get stuck, but we also had to be safe.

In the end, we decided we would prepare the boat to leave the following day, but we would not make a final decision until we had checked the weather forecast again in the morning. That kept our options open. It also meant we would be ready if we did decide to try to beat the bad weather that was coming straight down from the Arctic through the Labrador Sea.

Throughout the afternoon as Andy, now rested, pottered around the boat, doing various maintenance tasks, I mulled over the issues. Mick and I were almost certain we should get a good night's sleep and leave at first light in the morning. The forecast was not that bad, and my instinct was to keep moving.

It would be great to stay in St Mary's a bit longer and spend time with the people there, but we all knew we needed to be well across the worst of the Labrador Sea before the strong winds reached our latitude. Conditions of Force Four to Five over the next two days were a reasonable option.

I felt confident we would be OK. My only concern was that this was such a crucial leg to get right, and I knew there would be no room for error once we were 400 miles offshore. It would be too late. I had never been anything like that far from land before. The furthest I had been was about 50 miles and even that had felt very exposed. I reached for the Dictaphone, and spoke . . .

I'm still feeling tired, and I'm apprehensive. I'm not sure about the forecast. It's awkward whether to go before the bad stuff or to wait. It's the toughest call yet.

I remember Annabel, my sister-in-law, telling me before we left that I would have to make some hard decisions out here as leader – and this is one of them.

I miss Shara and little Jesse; I really miss us just being together, especially at times like this.

I feel edgy and vulnerable when there are these difficult choices to be made, especially as the person leading the team. I just want to keep everyone together and happy, and to make the right decisions. I hope I can.

Later on I spoke to Chloë again on the SAT phone. She had received a phone call from Mary, Mick's girlfriend. It was bad news. Mary's father had suddenly passed away. It had happened the hour we had left Halifax. I found Mick prepping his kit and told him to telephone Mary. I warned him it wasn't good news. Mick was devastated, but also torn. Torn between the team and wishing he could be there for Mary at this awful time.

Mary broke down and cried. Her father had just fallen

from the cliff of life, and Mick, her boyfriend, was now treading precariously near the edge. It all became too much for her later that day when she found an envelope. It was Mick's will, which he had written the day before he left. This was the final straw.

Mick and I spoke for a while, partly about Mary, partly about what to do now. We were trying to rationalize everything, but soon we were interrupted by a familiar voice.

'So we're all looking forward to seeing you tonight.'

It was Mayor Rumbolt again, extending the warm hand of hospitality, inviting us to an occasion at the town hall where, it seemed, we were to be the guests of honour.

'We would like to initiate you all as honorary Labradoreans,' he grinned. That sounded worrying. I had done initiations in the army, and they were rarely good news. Ever.

'Um . . . yep, that would be a pleasure,' I said.

The words tumbled out. We had all planned on an early night but it would have been ungracious to turn him down.

'We'll go along for a short time, show our faces and present the mayor with a decent bottle of whisky as a thanks for all he has done, and then bed,' I told the others.

As it was, they were all much keener to go than me. 'It'll be fun,' Charlie added.

So we went.

Everybody was in high spirits as we approached the house where we had been asked to meet before going on to what Alton cheerfully referred to as the 'town hall'. The guys were now in the frame of mind to celebrate our progress so far.

'They've got pretty good roads for such a small place,' Nige noted as we walked along.

'I know,' Charlie added, 'especially when you think they only go round the town and that's it. They don't actually lead anywhere. There is no road from here to Toronto, or any-where for that matter. The only way out of here is by plane or sea.'

We arrived at the house, full of festive fishermen, and found the beer flowing fast. The local people could not have been more friendly, and they made us feel quite proud when they said they could hardly believe we had travelled up from Nova Scotia in our small, yellow 32-foot rigid inflatable boat.

'You must go easy from now on, mind,' said another Rumbolt. 'You are heading into difficult waters from here on.'

Another asked, 'When are you leaving?'

I replied that we would probably leave the following day, and this remark provoked a chorus of amazement.

'You can't do that. It's northerly winds,' the fishermen said. 'We never go out in northerlies.'

'Really?' Andy asked.

'No, never.'

The locals were absolutely adamant, and I sensed eyes glancing in my direction.

'Why not?' I asked.

'The northerlies are the vicious ones,' they said. 'They blow onshore and come straight from the Arctic. They're cold and dangerous. It's a rule in our fleet. When the wind is a northerly, we wait for the winds to change.'

Above. My late dad Mickey Grylls and me aged eight

Right. My reason for coming home: Shara, my wife, with Jesse on the deck of our barge the day of his christening

The expedition's patron, HRH Prince of Wales with (from left to right) Eric Loth (from The British Masters Arnold & Son, our lead sponsors), Nigel Thompson, Mick Crosthwaite, Lt Andy Leivers, me and Jean-Marie Florent (also from our lead sponsors)

Into the Unknown by George Lewis. The oil painting was in aid of The Prince's Trust. *(Courtesy of Octavian Art)*

ARNOLD & SON
MASTERS OF THE LONGITUDE IN LONDON SINCE 1764
TransAtlantic Arctic Expedition 2003
Patron: HRH Prince of Wales

The *Arnold & Son Explorer*, looking a fraction of her beautiful self,
being lowered into Canadian waters for the first time

HMS *Newcastle* in heavy seas. Andy getting a perspective on what
lies ahead for us in an open boat

Left.
Leaving Halifax,
Nova Scotia.
The journey
begins

Below. Arriving at
night in Glace Bay,
Nova Scotia

Looking aft as we enter the sea-fog off Newfoundland, south of the
Belle Isle Strait

The remote coastline of Newfoundland, and one of the many lighthouses

Left. Bear in St Mary's harbour, Labrador

Below. The crew stare worriedly at the dark weather clouds ahead, with no idea of what we were going into

Sea-fog and swell off the Labrador coast

Charlie 'Lone Ranger' Laing, our brilliant cameraman

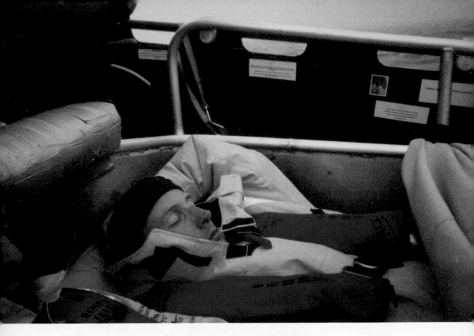

Trying to rest in our 'sardine tin'

The product of having soaking wet, freezing hands for days on end:
the bath effect!

It made sense, but I tried to rationalize the situation.

First, I told myself, the fishermen were dealing with conditions maybe 50 miles, maximum 100 miles, offshore. We had to think bigger. We were trying to get it right for over 700 miles straight across this ocean. That made the decision a different call altogether. We had to see the whole picture.

Second, the thought did cross my mind that it wasn't every day they have visitors, and that, even with Charlie and Nige's terrible jokes, they might not want us to leave quite so soon. At the very least, our arrival had broken their routine.

It was soon eleven o'clock, the time when I had promised myself we would all be back asleep in our beds, but the evening was only just starting. Mayor Rumbolt announced it was time to move on and join the rest of the folks at the town hall. We arrived, and quickly realized not only that almost the entire town was present but also that the night's entertainment seemed to be . . . us.

There was no escape from this local kindness, so I decided I might as well enter into the spirit of the occasion. We got drinks and I even had a dance with Mrs Rumbolt . . . although I wasn't sure exactly which Mrs Rumbolt I was dancing with.

We were soon led to a kind of wooden stage where, in preparation for our initiation as honorary Labradoreans, we were told to get dressed in chest-high boots, aprons, hair-nets and long rubber gloves, and to carry a crab net round our midriffs.

This was looking bad.

Amid hoots of laughter from the assembled crowd, who

were all having the time of their lives, we were asked to drink down pints of home-brewed beer and eat hunks of bread dipped in some very suspect-looking local paste. On top of all this, and at the same time, we had to sing a song.

And this was just the warm-up.

We were each then handed a clearly rotting sardine and told to eat it, head and all. Things were getting out of hand. We all hesitated, but Mick decided he had definitely had enough.

'Listen, Bear, I'm all for being a good sport, but this is getting ridiculous,' he said, suddenly looking very serious. 'If we eat this sort of thing, we could all get sick for days. I hate to say it, but our mission is to complete this expedition, not to be initiated as a Labradorean, nice as it is. We have to be sensible here.'

He was right. Andy, Charlie and Mick were able tactfully to toss the sardines to one side, but Nige and I were the last in line, and people were watching us very closely. There was no escape, so I looked at Nige, took a deep breath, and together we bit the heads off the revolting sardines and chewed.

We eventually managed to leave at 1.30 a.m. 'Give me the sea over the sardines any day,' I told Mick as we finally reached our hotel room.

Our plan remained to leave at 6 a.m., so long as the final weather forecast was all right. Whatever our doubts about the wind and a beam sea, whatever the local fishermen said, the bottom line was that worse weather was on the way. If we waited we would get caught in it for certain.

We had forty-eight hours' clear weather ahead of us, and I believed we could handle the Force Five winds if they did happen to come early.

I tossed around my bed sleeplessly. Wondering. Questioning. Then finally, thankfully, out of exhaustion, I fell asleep.

7. UNSEEN CREW

Man must live by faith – faith in himself,
and faith in others.

Anon.

Everyone was awake by 4.30 in the morning after our initiation at St Mary's, ready to set out on the second-longest leg of the entire voyage, just over 700 miles straight across the Labrador Sea. We checked the weather forecast. It was still no change, and by 6 a.m. we were on our way.

Once again, Canadian hospitality had been so warm. It was sad to be finally leaving these shores and lovely to see a small group of the locals gathered on the jetty, even so early in the morning, to wave goodbye.

As we left, I had passed Alton a sack of surplus chocolates for his fishing trips, and we were all shouting thanks to him across the water. It was a lovely moment, but I did feel rather bad when I realized later that by mistake I had also included in Alton's goodie bag a leftover medical kit of Carol's.

It was not just any old medical kit. It was a personal enema kit that Carol, for some bizarre reason, had deemed indispensable. Alton was going to get the shock of his life when he rummaged through the bag on a cold fishing trip looking for a Mars bar.

None the less, everything was going smoothly, and all of us felt a surge of confidence and excitement. We were moving through a beautiful part of the world, down the narrow inlet from St Mary's to Battle Harbour, past rolling mountains on either side, through the now familiar strong scent of heather and fir trees. The water was mirror calm, and I recall thinking to myself that there was nowhere in the world where I would rather be at this moment than right here with these four guys. It was magical and free.

Andy was checking the engine; Mick had been on the SAT phone, getting a final up-to-date forecast from Mike Town; Nige had been punching in the new waypoints on the plotter; and Charlie was checking the waterproofing on his camera. Everyone was getting on with their specific tasks, and everyone was feeling strong.

We had no idea how much we would need our strength.

Privately, I felt as though I had been tested back in St Mary's, and had managed to pull through with a tough decision. I felt certain it was right to go. Even as we cruised down the inlet, I was running over the logic again: the fishermen said the northerly winds were bad, but they had also talked about the sea being full of ice; we had to take the weather windows when they became available, and the immediate forecast was not bad.

I spoke into the Dictaphone:

I just want to get the first twenty-four hours of this leg out of the way. That could be the tough time because we are heavy with fuel and so slow and vulnerable to big seas. We need a day and night's grace before we hit the big stuff; that's when we will need all our power and manoeuvrability. There is an element of risk and unpredictability in all this. I know that, but I just hope and pray we have made the right decision.

With that, I flicked the stop button on the recorder and took a piece of paper, wrapped in plastic, out of my grab bag. On this I had written out one particular verse from the Bible.

Nicky Gumbel is another squash friend of mine in London; he also happens to be a priest. Everyone at the gym simply calls him 'the Pope'. It makes us laugh. Nicky had phoned me as I was checking in my luggage at Heathrow, and given me a little verse that he and his wife Pippa had felt strongly that morning applied to me. It had lifted my spirits then as it did now when I read it leaving Labrador.

When you walk through the waters, they shall not pass over you. I have saved you. I have called you by name. You are precious in my eyes.

(Isaiah 43:2)

That was good to know. I read it again, took a deep breath and tucked it away in my bag. I remember a famous round-the-world sailor once saying, 'There's no such thing as an atheist in the Arctic Ocean.' I had always liked that. It had soul.

We duly passed Battle Harbour and headed out northeast into the Labrador Sea, the stretch of water I had read so much about. As we advanced we felt noticeably colder air on our faces. The next land we would see would be Greenland.

I had done my fair share of reading in advance of the expedition, and this research included a science journal which had described these particular waters as follows:

The Labrador Current originates in western Greenland. The outflow from Hudson Strait combines with the Baffin Island Current to become the Labrador Current. This Labrador Current travels 1–2 knots an hour, and carries with it pack ice, cold water and icebergs.

It was one of these icebergs that sank the *Titanic* off the Grand Banks in 1912. Upwards of 10,000 bergs are released each year, as many as 1,300 bergs from Greenland's Jacobshavener Glacier alone. The bergs slowly disintegrate as they are carried south from Baffin Bay, and a grand spectacle of about 2,500 giant ice chunks parade past the Labrador coast each year. More than half of these icebergs pass the Belle Isle Strait, and this whole area poses a substantial hazard to shipping, particularly when the area is thick with the Labrador's prevalent sea fog.

Nobody could say we hadn't been warned but we were only half a mile out from the coastline, when I noticed something strange.

'Hold on.'

'What?'

'This wind is not quite a northerly. It's coming from more north-east. It's going to give us a head sea. Look at the waves already beginning.'

In layman's terms, the waves were not rolling across us, they were building and rolling directly towards us. Already laden down with full tanks of fuel for the long crossing, we now faced the harsh reality of heading straight into the waves and weather.

My instant reaction was that we should turn back, retreat to St Mary's and revise our plans. These were not the conditions that we had expected, the conditions upon which we had based all our calculations. A different wind and a different kind of sea meant we would be playing a completely different game.

Then I looked at the waves. They were pretty small, just gentle rollers. They didn't look that bad, and the wind was steady. We were expecting it to strengthen significantly over the next twenty-four hours or so, but not unmanageably.

We all had a quick word together, to discuss the situation. It was not ideal but, we agreed, no reason to retreat. We were on our way and all of us were hungry to get this leg done.

Our spirits were raised soon afterwards by the sighting of our first big whale, spouting magnificently on the port side, and within the hour we had passed another massive, majestic iceberg. If we had been passengers aboard a big cruise ship, we would have been able to sit back and savour the Arctic wonders. That would have been great, gin and tonic in hand. Instead, we were perched on our open RIB, anxiously studying the state of the wind and waves, trying to predict the future.

We didn't like what we saw. Hour by hour, unmistakably, the conditions were deteriorating.

The swell was building slowly and the temperature was dropping fast. By mid-afternoon we were in full gear: waterproofs, two balaclavas, gloves and helmets. Each of us was working hard to stay warm. We had given up trying to stay dry.

The boat was hitting the waves head-on now. Every wave was steep and sharp. They were pitching us up about ten feet as they connected, then crashing down on top of us – over and over again. Each time we were lifted up we braced ourselves, tensing every muscle; and each time we slammed back down every bone in our bodies shuddered with the impact. We winced on contact.

By late afternoon the light was fading and the temperature was still dropping. I was shivering uncontrollably. This was not good. It wasn't even night yet. I looked around at the others. Some were lying in the sardine tin, eyes closed. Charlie was awake but he was shivering too. We had to do something before it got dark, otherwise we would freeze to death.

'Stop the boat, Andy,' I said, tapping his shoulder. 'People are getting really cold, me included. We need our final layers.'

The boat lolled about in the swell. We could no longer see land and the sea was a dark and menacing grey.

The two guys who had all the kit on, every last fleece, seemed to be managing. They weren't as cold as us three. I had wanted to wait until it got dark and much colder before putting on my last fleece layer, but that time had come sooner than expected. My hands were shaking.

'Mick, can you help me get this zip undone on my drysuit?' I asked him urgently. 'It's jammed.'

It had also started to rain steadily.

He undid the zip, fed the fleece over my head and pulled the arms down sharply.

'Thanks, buddy,' I muttered as he helped rezip the drysuit over me. Then we both checked Charlie. He was looking warmer.

Cold is so dangerous and this was a different sort of cold to that found on high mountains. This was a constant damp, wet cold that penetrated everything. Everest might have been technically colder, but it was not so all-consuming. The temperature there might drop to −40 degrees, but it was powder-dry. Nothing ever got the chance to melt. This was different: it was not so far below zero but it was wet, and, with the constant wind chill of 20 knots forward speed plus the head wind, it got bitingly cold. And the wind and wet got in everywhere.

Now we were wearing everything we possessed. If any of us got cold now, there was nothing else to rely on.

We were soon under way again, sticking to our rota, but nothing seemed straightforward any more. Helming became much more difficult because it was now imperative to keep the boat straight into the oncoming waves. But our course was just off that angle. That meant we had to weave our way forward, bringing the nose back into the sea when the waves were breaking ahead of us.

Navigating was awkward because it was difficult to follow the course when the instruments were being continually covered in spray. When it was your turn to rest in the sardine tin, all you could do was huddle under the tarpaulin and curl up in a ball to try to keep warm.

I heard a murmur next to me. Nige rolled towards me and spoke through his helmet.

'Just think, we could be in the old speedboat I had in

Poole. Remember? The one that almost sank when a yacht went by, where you would get swamped by a ripple. Just imagine how that little boat would have coped out here.'

Nige chuckled at the thought, then was forced back again as he braced against another wave. This was Nige through and through. His approach helped keep us all smiling at many hard moments, in spite of genuinely miserable conditions.

Each of us was feeling tired as darkness fell. We had been hoping for a break from the relentless head seas but through the night they gradually built up even more. Hour by hour, shifting through the rota, we just focused on the next wave, concentrating, surviving, advancing out to sea.

The violence with which the boat crashed off the waves as they disappeared under us was exhausting, but one factor debilitated us more than anything: the incessant wet, the feeling of being continually drenched, over and over again. Each time a wave broke across the boat, we were covered in gallons and gallons of icy water, and absolutely everything was getting soaked. Every few seconds we'd hit another wave, and wherever we were in the boat, the spray would wash over us. We'd close our eyes as the salt water trickled down the inside of our visors, down our cheeks, into our mouths and around our neck seals.

Every bag and tarpaulin was drenched. I opened the watertight zip of my grab bag to take another anti-seasickness pill, and a wave flooded the bag. The pills became soaked and crumbly. The zips were going brown from rust after just a few days.

The sound of water was everywhere, an incessant dripping. It was like living in an open-top car in a car wash, in a washing machine, in a deep-freeze.

Icy water seeped down our arms into our gloves. These were properly sealed diving gloves, but still, after twenty-four hours of such conditions, they were sodden and cold like everything else.

As we ploughed on through the night, some of us were starting to feel sick. Even Andy was struggling. The familiar cure of fixing your gaze on the horizon didn't apply here because there was no horizon, just blackness. Alton Rumbolt's wife had kindly given us a round of crab sandwiches in St Mary's, but the stench of them, soaked in diesel and salt water, made us all want to retch. I threw them overboard, apologizing.

By morning, after twenty-four hours at sea, we were exhausted. We had set out from St Mary's aware that we were trying to cross the Labrador in a tight window of decent weather. I still believed we had made the correct decision, but the predicted wind direction had turned out to be wrong and that small window had been dramatically tightened.

I looked around the boat, at Mick and Andy, Charlie and Nige. Everybody was focused. We had one common aim: to reach Greenland and safety. But Greenland was still over 400 miles off and, on the chart, Labrador still looked only a blip away. This was going to be a real struggle and every glance down at the chart-plotter while on watch told us the same story. We were making perilously slow progress.

At times, you would come off watch and the estimated 'time to destination' dial would say 'two days, eighteen hours and forty-one minutes'. By the next time you were navigating, four hours later, you hoped that the time remaining would be significantly less. But often it was more. If our speed dropped only slightly due to the conditions, the 'time to destination' dial would rise dramatically. It would now say 'three days, eleven hours and ten minutes'. This was so demoralizing. We should have covered the dial.

In those dark hours curled up in a ball in the pouring rain, shivering, I often thought of home and our unseen crew, which for me was my dad. It wasn't advice I was after, or even guidance, it was just comfort, a familiar, warm hand to hold.

Mickey Grylls was born on 21 February 1934, and he died on 7 February 2001, only a couple of weeks before his sixty-seventh birthday. He was a true gentleman: a family man, a man of faith and a kind soul.

To me, he was always just Dad, and that was enough. And on this wild, grey, windy North Atlantic morning, 300 miles from anywhere, I peered from the sardine tin out across the endless sea and remembered him.

Silly things, like the dewdrop that used to hang from the end of his nose when he was walking in the cold; the coarse stubble when he hadn't shaved; the warm kiss; the smiling pride in his eyes when I achieved something ... anything. And his laughter.

There was that poem that my father loved so much, written by a soldier just before a battle during the English Civil War. 'Oh Lord, you know how busy I must be this day,' he wrote. 'If I forget you, I pray do not forget me.' I could see the poem where it always sat, wedged in the frame of his mirror.

The second verse of Dad's favourite hymn, 'I vow to thee, my country,' said it all. It was him in a nutshell, although he never knew it.

> And there's another country, I've heard of long ago,
> Most dear to them that love her, most great to them that
>   know;
> We may not count her armies, we may not see her King;
> Her fortress is a faithful heart, her pride is suffering;
> And soul by soul and silently her shining bounds increase,
> And her ways are ways of gentleness,
> And all her paths are peace.

I missed him so much. In these difficult moments particularly, I so wished he could be here with me.

It was early morning at our barge on the Thames. We were just getting up. There was a knock on the door. It was a policeman. That was strange. Shara sat beside me as he told me my father had died. My mother was many hours away and so the police were asked to tell me. The officer did so, and with great gentleness. I even thanked him for his time. I was completely numb.

Then going with Shara to the funeral directors, to give

them my dad's favourite boxer shorts to be buried in. I held them in my hand feeling ridiculous. But I couldn't even do it. I was unable to go into the funeral parlour. I tried three times but instead broke down with Shara in the alleyway outside.

Then, at 2 a.m. at my parents' home, sitting beside his coffin the night before the funeral, alone. Laying his old Royal Marine beret on the coffin. Afraid. Afraid of how I would cope in this world without him.

Then finally, carrying his coffin down the aisle of the church, flanked by five of my closest friends in the world – Ed Amies, Mick Crosthwaite, Trucker Goodwin-Hudson, Charlie Mackesy and Hugo Mackenzie-Smith – our arms linked, being literally held by their strength. How I needed them. All I could hear was the strange, hollow click of our shoes down the aisle. Dad felt so heavy.

He had written a reading for me to do at Shara's father's funeral. I read it again at my dad's funeral only a few months later. The words were so tender, and had turned out to be so prophetic.

This was what he wrote:

I have passed on.
Remember my time with you.
Treasure all those moments together,
Those moments of fun and laughter;
As you remember, know that I am with you.
It is not the number of years we live that counts,
It's how we live that matters.
As you live your lives, remember I am with you.

Build on the beliefs we created together.
Hold on to that which is right.
Discard all that is wrong.
When you are happy, know that I am with you.
When you are sad or in pain, know that I am with you.
True love does not need a physical presence;
What is called death is no more than the removal of the
    physical being.
Now that I have passed on I understand it all.
I am hand in hand with our Lord, yet I am with you.

The words were so simple: 'When you are in pain, I am with you.' But was it true? Even out here? When I was afraid?

The words 'I am hand in hand with our Lord, yet I am with you.' But would you hold my hand now? Could I really believe in this 'Lord' of yours? Would you give me faith when it counted?

Andy was having the same kinds of feeling midway across the Labrador Sea. He had lost his father as well, but at a much younger age. That is harder. But I understood. Days later, he told me that he had asked his dad for help. He hadn't done that in years.

'Maybe that seagull is my dad,' Andy had mused, looking at one of the birds following us.

He smiled at the thought, hoping he was right.

None of the crew was particularly religious. It was never really something that we discussed. Faith is very intimate, if it is to be real. For me, here on the Labrador Sea, alone and in terrifying conditions, my Christian faith was all I really had; not some sort of blind, all-conquering faith, but an intimate, at times faltering faith. The sort that says I'm not quite sure about everything, especially the very 'religious' bits, but I love the sound of this Jesus. The one my dad knew.

Faith is always a risk, just like love. It has taken me a long time to admit this, but I am no longer frightened to say I need it. I need that comfort. I often feel lost, but my faith says I'm never lost to Him. That means the world to me, and faith is a risk I want always to take. At the end of the day, it's all I have.

C. S. Lewis once wrote about this Jesus: 'Safe? Who said anything about safe? 'Course he isn't safe. But he's good.'

Dad would have agreed with that.

To me, faith is not about us. It's about Him. It is about being loved and about being held, unconditionally, regardless of how well or badly we may be doing.

This Jesus always seems so much bigger than me, so much stronger than all my self-doubt and fears. He has this habit of stealing in when I least expect Him, and always when I least deserve it. When I am right at my wits' end, when I feel I am losing the precious hope we all need so dearly. These are the moments when I sense Him near me, and I can never quite believe it. He never condemns, He just sustains. He doesn't judge, He understands. He gives me my hope again, and says be brave. He helps me when I most need it.

Why does this love mean so much to me? Maybe because I don't expect it. Because I don't deserve it. It just comes, regardless. It is like the sea and the waves and the tides.

You can't keep God out. He's all around us, if we're just still enough to listen.

'Do not be terrified; do not be discouraged, for the Lord your God will be with you wherever you go.' A man called Joshua in the Bible heard God say that, and he went on to lead a nation.

Faith does this. It hopes. It holds us. It feels like home and I'm lost without it.

Dad wrote that he was 'with me'. I hope every night that this is true. Whether I am kneeling beside Jesse's cot or out on the ocean or on some mountain, I pray for this always. For Dad and my Jesus to be right beside me.

And right here, right now, in the waves and wind, I knew that, somehow, the unseen crew were at our side.

8. RUNNING ON VAPOUR

There can only be true courage when first there is genuine fear.

Dr David Livingstone

Andy was sitting bolt upright in the sardine tin.

I didn't know why.

More than thirty hours into this bone-shuddering, relentless storm, the winds were still at fever pitch, and the 20-foot waves were now coming at us head-on. Each wave was taking us further and deeper into the heart of the storm. We had no choice but to hang on, clinging to the routine by which we would stay afloat and continue this painfully slow progress across the Labrador Sea.

But Andy sitting bolt upright in the sardine tin was not part of this routine.

In these harrowing conditions, we had adapted the rota so that while two of us would stay at the console, one helming and the other navigating, the other three would squeeze into the sardine tin. We would spoon, body to body, trying awkwardly to get some rest and shelter beneath the tarpaulin sheet. Three of us in the sardine tin together meant we kept warmer.

But Andy was sitting bolt upright, staring out to sea. Water was still crashing over his head, but he hardly moved.

Something was wrong. I knew it.

A minute later I looked again.

Andy was up now, checking the fuel gauges, pressing the dial, taking a reading, looking up, checking the gauges again. I couldn't see the expression on his face through his helmet, but his slow, deliberate body language suggested he was agitated and concerned.

When Andy was happy, I knew it; he would be wearing his Peruvian woollen hat, eating with his green plastic spoon, cosy in his own cocoon, at peace with the world. That was a very different Andy to now.

Still the wind licked across the boat, and the incessant waves were crashing over the bows and console every thirty seconds or so. The sea just didn't seem to care. It had no regard for our struggles. The waves just roared towards us with a deafening mass of white water; then our world would drop away under us. One wave was gone and the next would be upon us.

Looking behind me, I was stunned by the speed at which the waves were racing away from us, and the sheer energy and force by which they travelled, unhindered, unbridled. They were like wild horses galloping.

Even the most basic kinds of communication and move-ment had become almost impossible. I wanted to turn to Andy and ask him if there was a problem. But this was not easily done. I could only watch him through my visor.

Andy recalls:

My responsibility was to make sure the fuel and engine systems worked efficiently, but it wasn't easy because the weather had such an impact on how fast we burnt through the fuel.

In planning each leg of the expedition, I tried to take account of this uncertainty by loading at least 20 per cent more fuel than was necessary. But the legs were so long and the boat so relatively small that there wasn't physically room for much greater margin.

During the storm in the Labrador Sea, when we were still about 300 miles off Greenland, I started to get concerned. The head sea meant we were on 2,600 engine revs, moving forward at only 12 knots. It was dangerously inefficient and our fuel reserves were running low. I did a calculation – back-of-a-fag-packet stuff – and worked out that at this rate we would run dry between 100 and 150 miles short of Greenland. I couldn't see how we could narrow this and still make any progress.

I checked and rechecked the levels; I was worried. Our lives were not imminently in danger if we could get a Mayday off; the Danish icebreakers could get to us in a day possibly, but it would have been so gutting if we ran out of fuel and had to abandon the expedition. This was my area of responsibility and I would have felt as if I had let everyone down.

So much preparation: two years' worth of Bear's and the others' work, and it would have been my fault. And what a bloody stupid way to fail – running out of juice.

I waited a further minute and then finally Andy beckoned me over. We stood side by side, braced against the constant pitching of the boat, shouting to each other to make ourselves heard above the wind and waves.

'Bear, we're running short on fuel,' Andy yelled.

'How bad is it?'

'Pretty bad. We're struggling.'

'Well, what can we do to reduce our burn rate?'

'We need to reduce our speed. That's the only way of making the fuel last longer.'

'Reduce it to what?'

'Eight knots.'

'Eight knots?'

'Yeah, I know it's crazy, but it's our only choice.'

It didn't take me long to work out the consequences of slowing to 8 knots. It would mean that from this point it would take us another thirty-six hours to reach Greenland instead of the twenty hours we were expecting. We would be off the planing speed and the boat would be very vulnerable, completely at the mercy of the sea. We would hardly have the speed to push through these big head seas. Everyone was freezing cold and soaking wet, and I knew this would now take our struggle up to a new level. I wasn't sure we could cope with a further thirty-six hours like this.

But we had no option.

'If we do this, will we make Greenland?' I asked.

'Touch and go . . . but if the seas die down a bit, well, then we should make it . . . just,' he replied.

'OK, do it.'

I turned and gazed across the restless grey ocean, trying to keep calm. We had been confronted by a major problem, and we had taken prompt, decisive action, but I was still deeply worried.

The prospect of aborting the expedition because we ran out of fuel haunted me. It would not go down as a very glamorous failure. It would be a stark, brutal waste of two years' planning; gone – just like that.

The bottom line was this: we needed a break in the weather. Given some decent conditions, we would almost certainly get to Greenland. However, if the winds and the head seas remained as strong as they were, there would probably be nothing we could do to avoid calling the rescue services.

We needed help.

Not for the first time, I tried to pray. Truly pray.

Anyone looking out of the window of a jumbo jet flying overhead would never even see us down here. We were so small and insignificant in this unforgiving sea. We were effectively invisible. Tiny. Lost in a sea of white horses.

'Please, God,' I prayed, eyes closed, 'I know it is asking for quite a big one, but please make these seas go calm.'

I was waiting, eyes squeezed shut. A few moments passed – as long as I dared – before I slowly opened my eyes, looking for the miracle; but there was none.

I wondered how many times through the centuries God must have heard this same prayer from men fighting for their lives at sea. Thousands. I knew this. But I prayed again.

Massive amounts of water were still pouring over the boat. We were being drenched by the spray, and the RIB was really labouring against the giant waves. The engine would peak, and then seem to stall as the boat was suspended in mid-air as it dropped off the back of a steep wave. We would all cling on, motionless, until we landed, often on our side, with a crash. Then, instantly, the engine would pick up revs again. Its computer system would be carefully monitoring the impact and revs. I had no idea how the hell it was still working but it was, and slowly we were edging towards Greenland.

Most of us had not eaten anything for twenty-four hours, partly because we were feeling so sick but also because it was impossible to eat when the boat was being thrown around so violently. Andy said it was like trying to eat while sitting on a fairground rollercoaster ride. Just the thought of cold, salt water-soaked Lancashire hotpot and baked beans made me retch. We just accepted the reality that in a storm, eating anything more than the odd flapjack was almost impossible.

Drinking was just as hard, but more important. No matter how bad we were feeling, we had to drink. Charlie was sick again over the side of the boat. Then he laboured over to the jerry can to refill his water bottle to drink. It was a horrible task.

I squeezed into the sardine tin, so tight against Mick that I could feel the zip on his dry-suit back pressing against me. I put the Dictaphone's watertight pouch to my mouth . . .

We seem to have been going for ever; then I look at the chart and see we've still got hundreds of miles to Greenland. I'm not sure if we can keep going like this. Everything is so wet. My head is freezing, as my balaclava has been continually drenched for almost two days and nights.

Our dry-suits are being amazing and I have no idea how the hell they are keeping this amount of water out. But still inevitably water gets in, all down your legs. This happens when your zip is undone to try to pee, or when you stretch out at the wrong time and break the seal on your wrists or neck. This sea is just so cold and so penetrating.

Nige's lifejacket has just gone off. These lifejackets are very high-spec commercial ones and they are supposed to inflate only when you are in the water. Nige's has just gone off in the sardine tin. That's how sodding wet it is in here.

These seas are ferocious. We are into deeper ocean now, so that means the waves should become longer and it should be more comfortable. But there's no sign of that yet. It is just black all around us. I am cold and damp, and I am just dreaming of Greenland with each bit of salt water I taste.

We were approaching the end of our second day on the Labrador Sea, and the North Atlantic was doing what the North Atlantic does best. Creating chaos. Andy understood the seriousness of the situation. 'I'm not a very religious person,' he would recall later, 'but I lay in the sardine tin that night and prayed. I prayed that my late dad would help us with the weather. I might not be a huge believer in God, but I believed in my dad, and I knew we needed help from somewhere.'

As dusk approached, we checked all the gauges again and ran through the calculations. We were burning only 70 litres of fuel per hour, compared to 90 litres per hour earlier, and we had only lost one knot of speed. That was encouraging, but reaching Greenland was still going to be touch and go.

Everyone knew the plain facts. If the sea died down a

bit we stood a real chance of making it. But in our heart of hearts we all knew that if the weather conditions did not improve, we would almost certainly have no chance of getting there. Now, forty hours into the storm, and still with no sign of reprieve, everyone sensed that rescue was beginning to look like the most likely outcome. We were powerless to do anything more.

We simply weren't getting any breaks in these conditions. The seas were still running wild and huge.

The physical battering was taking its toll. Every twenty minutes or so we all made a point of looking around the boat, checking how the person next to us was coping. I had started to suspect that all of us, including me, were suffering from the early stages of hypothermia. Our reactions were more sluggish than usual, and it felt impossible to concentrate on anything. We were drained and we were cold. Even the most straightforward tasks – whether it was checking the fuel gauges, tying a knot or just having a pee – now took on the dimensions of a major undertaking.

But I needed to pee. I tried to stave it off. To perform even this simple task was a nightmare. I tried to block it in my mind. Ten minutes later, I knew I had to go. I clambered out of the sardine tin and tried to steady myself against the console.

The drill normally was to go to the stern of the RIB, harness on so that you felt confident enough to use both hands to undo the dry-suit zip, and then pee. But in these conditions, to move even that far around the boat was dangerous and unnecessary. I wedged myself between the console side and the sardine tin and started to fumble with my dry-suit zip.

A wave crashed over the back of me and I frantically grabbed the edge of the console. I steadied myself again and tried to hold on with one hand and undo my fly with the other. It was impossible. In desperation, I realized there was only one way to pee in these conditions: kneeling down.

I crouched down on the floor and using my elbows as a brace, I found I could hold myself steady against the violent motion of the waves. I undid the zip and peed on the floor. Another wave poured over and washed it away in seconds. I spat the salt water from my mouth and clambered back alongside Nige.

To do 'number twos' in this sort of condition just wouldn't happen. It would be lethal. Most of us managed to crap in calm seas, hanging inelegantly off the back of the jet platform, but in this sort of sea it was unthinkable. Somehow our mindset and the adrenalin ensured we never needed to go when it was rough. I guess we weren't eating much, which helped. But looking back, it is strange how we managed to last out for days at a time.

Andy was helming now, but he was drowsy and veering wildly off his course. His head was drooping and he was struggling, although he was only twenty-five minutes into his shift. His concentration had gone and the waves that were smashing into the side of the RIB were hardly even drawing his attention. He was going down with exhaustion. To his credit, he recognized this. He turned to Charlie and asked him to take over. He couldn't focus his eyes. The chart plotter had become a blur to him. He needed Charlie to help him this time.

This kind of gesture takes real courage, but it was what I had wanted from the team all along: an honesty, a humanity, a willingness to be vulnerable and draw on our strengths together. That was what made us stronger. Collectively, we were always going to be better than when we were on our own.

I had no doubt that Charlie himself would need Andy's help sooner or later, but for now it was Andy's turn to need that help. They swapped helm and the boat carried on into the waves.

But all our bodies were slowing down, and I for one was shivering. I had seen hypothermia among climbers high on Everest, and I knew that there was not much we could do. We just needed that break in the weather.

But that wasn't happening, and with every minute that passed, we seemed to be drawing nearer and nearer to the moment I had been dreading, the moment when we called for help. It would be my decision, and a terrible one to make.

'We shouldn't leave it too late,' Mick told me sensibly at one stage. 'I mean, if this is the situation, well, there's no point waiting until we have run out of fuel before we put out a Mayday. We don't want to be floating around for a day with no power. We can at least put them on standby and let them know our position.'

He was right. It was logical.

It was just that I didn't want to face it.

'OK,' I said, relenting in the face of common sense. 'I'm going to call Chloë and just let her know what's happening.'

Mick nodded. 'She does need to be informed,' he affirmed. 'It gives us a backup if we do run out of fuel.'

I agreed. 'Slow the boat right down, will you, Nige?' I asked.

Whenever we wanted to use the SAT phone, we had to reduce our speed to a knot or two. Then one of us was able to crawl on hands and knees into the tiny cramped console, under the helm position, in order to dial. This space was jammed with spares, food and supplies; it was dark and stank of leaking diesel. It was a miserable place on land, in a big sea it was hell. Idling along at just 1 knot keeping the boat head to sea made her loll about awkwardly. Most of us would start feeling sick. These calls needed to be made as quickly as possible.

I crawled inside on all-fours, banging my head on the metal hatch. I cursed. Nige swung his feet out of the way to let me crawl past. I took off my diving gloves. My hands were shaking as I pulled out the SAT phone and began to unwrap it from its plastic bag. I fumbled to attach the charger, then the antenna wire. Time was ticking on. I could hear my own breathing – it was nervous and rapid. I could also hear Charlie being sick again. More than any of us, he hated having to stop the boat.

I carefully dialled Chloë's number in London, holding

the phone a few inches from my soaking head in an effort to keep it dry. This phone was our lifeline, and needed to be kept out of the water at all costs. I waited.

Nothing. No dial tone.

Lying half in and half out of this tiny hatch, desperately trying to stop my head banging on the metal rails on the console roof inches above me, I dialled again. Still nothing.

'Bloody work,' I cursed at the phone.

Finally, on the fourth try, I heard a telephone ringing far away in London, in a different world, a warm and comfortable place where all was safe and dry and OK, a world away from here.

'Hello, Chloë?'

'Hi, Bear, how are you?' she replied, bright and breezy.

'Get a pen and paper,' I told her. 'We're in trouble.'

It was around eight in the evening in London, and Chloë seemed to be in a restaurant somewhere. I could hear noises behind her. She was back in seconds. 'Go for it,' she said.

'Mick, I need our lat and longs,' I screamed to him. He would be able to read these off the plotter.

'Four-ah, two-ah, seven-ah.' Mick was shouting them in his loudest, most clipped voice. It made me smile. This sure had his concentration; Mick didn't want any errors here. I relayed the numbers on, shouting them out above the clamour of the wind. Chloë repeated them correctly. Then I told her we were running critically low on fuel.

'We've got about 1,200 litres of fuel left,' I shouted down the phone. 'We reckon that should last us for eighteen hours, and get us maybe 140 miles closer. Right now, we are 195 miles from Greenland in terrible conditions.'

'OK, I've got that,' Chloë said. Her tone of voice had changed. She knew it was serious.

'One more thing,' I added. 'Please call Captain Pennefather and tell him what's happening. We're OK, and will call again when we reckon we have two hours' running time left.'

I replaced the SAT phone and wriggled back out of the hatch, trying to yank my gloves back on. Andy revved the engine, and we started to move again. We struggled on, the RIB crawling up and over the waves at a pathetic 9 knots.

Chloë was aware that Willie Pennefather was in Scotland, where, among other things, he was sorting out various aspects of our scheduled return to John O'Groats. She eventually tracked him down to Edinburgh.

Willie recalls:

I had left for Scotland on 2 August with a slight feeling of detachment from the expedition, although I had followed the crew's progress every day on the Internet. I had been invited to be part of the official party attending the Edinburgh Military Tattoo. It was a very formal occasion involving drinks and a black-tie dinner, before we were to travel in official cars with police outriders to Edinburgh Castle, arriving in time to allow us to be seated in the Royal Box at exactly the start of the display.

At dinner, the sergeant came to tell me that Chloë Boyes was on the telephone for me.

I told him to ask if I could ring her after dinner. I assumed it was to discuss the plans for the crew's return. The sergeant reported that after dinner would be OK, but said Chloë had sounded a bit alarmed.

I thought of leaving the table unseen, but my host General Nick Parker and his guests, General Sir Mike Jackson and Menzies Campbell among others, were not the type of people who would not have noticed. Thoughts of Sir Francis Drake and his game of bowls crossed my mind, but I eased out and called her back some fifteen minutes later.

She then dropped the bombshell.

'They are 200 miles west of Greenland in a gale,' she told me calmly, 'and Bear says they are critically close to running out of fuel. I don't know what to do.'

The next hour was frantic as I somehow tried to combine the jovialities and formalities of the Tattoo parade with also trying to instigate some rescue contingency plans. I found myself conducting analysis discussions with the London team at the desk of the GOC Scotland, then in the back of a car on the ADC's mobile phone, with flashing blue lights all around, then at the back of the Royal Box at Edinburgh Castle with pipes swirling in the background. It was strangely surreal to know that at this precise moment of such pomp and ceremony here in Edinburgh, these guys were struggling for their lives in a lonely, terrifying sea.

I must say I could easily watch the Edinburgh Tattoo again, having had my mind so firmly elsewhere! On this occasion, I could only think of the boys and what they were going through out there.

Our task was to do everything possible to prepare for whatever fate would decide was to happen.

We knew we could do no more than alert the rescue services,

keep them informed, and ensure Bear told us at least an hour before they ran out of fuel, so that they could be rescued from a boat which still had steerage – this could be critical if the weather was still atrocious. We also decided to keep the team's families in the dark for the time being, and to contact the Duty Fleet Controller at Northwood, who gave us vital access to the Naval Weather Centre.

All this done, I returned to the party, even if my thoughts were elsewhere.

Meanwhile, nothing was giving at all. We were still battling against the brutal ocean. Waves as large as houses kept thundering towards us, picking us up, dumping us down and soaking us in icy water. Perhaps it was the cold and fatigue, but I started to personify the waves. To me, as they flew past, they seemed to turn and look at us strangely, as if they were asking, 'What the hell are you doing out here in such a boat?'

I didn't have an answer. Then the wave was gone.

We were all becoming frightened and I knew it; we were so completely exposed and vulnerable, dangerously out of place.

I prayed again.

'Please, God, please calm these seas,' I said under my breath, lying in the sardine tin, hugging Mick in front of me not just to keep warm, but because I was scared. 'You've helped me so many times before, but I really need you now. I really need you to hear me. I really need you to help us.'

None of us had managed more than a brief doze over the past two days, and a couple of hours later I was helming again. For this particular shift, from 11 p.m. till midnight, Charlie and I sat shoulder to shoulder at the console, fighting to keep the boat on course and under control.

As I helmed, I noticed a small piece of coloured plastic flapping around on the anchor, attached to the foredeck. I knew it was some sort of Chinese lucky charm that a stranger had placed on the side of the boat while a bunch of well-wishers were crowding around us on the quay in Halifax, Canada. Most of them had draped flowers and things on the boat, but this particular woman had presented this small, peculiar token.

I saw her, and didn't really like the idea of the charm, but it would have been rude not to accept the gesture and I let it pass. I hadn't given it another thought until now – in trouble, so far out in the ocean. I began to wonder whether this could be the reason why God was not answering my prayers. Maybe this charm was keeping His goodness out. It sounds crazy and superstitious now, but right there, in the darkness, I was clutching at anything and praying like never before. I was desperate.

As the minutes passed, I felt compelled somehow to get rid of the charm. Everything might be OK then, I thought. The sea might die down. 'Just forget it and concentrate, Bear,' I told myself.

But the more I dismissed this idea as ridiculous, the more I believed it to be the case. And a minute later, it was all I could think about again. I couldn't take my eyes off this ruddy little plastic thing, swinging hypnotically with the motion of the bow.

The problem was, however, that it was wrapped around the anchor arm at the very front of the boat, and I knew that getting to that area would be extremely risky, especially while the boat was being thrown around in the storm. One slip on those slippery tubes, one awkward pitch of the boat, and I could easily be washed overboard. My lifeline should hold me, but at 10 knots, in the black of night, in these waves, I would be dragged until I drowned.

'Forget it,' I told myself. 'God might not like the charm, but He doesn't want to me drown either.'

I did forget about it.

For about thirty seconds.

Damn it, I had to get rid of that thing. Charlie hadn't noticed this and I didn't want to tell him what was on my mind. He would have said to stay put and that I was being irrational, which may have been true. So I made up a story about the sea anchor looking as if it was coming loose from its housing. That would do.

'Don't bother, Bear,' Charlie said. 'It's fine.'

'No,' I persisted. 'I'm going. Take the helm.'

So I slid from my seat and began to fumble for my harness. I swung myself over the edge of the console and began to edge, step by step, along the tubes, round to the front of the boat.

Once on the foredeck, I grabbed for the handholds and steadied myself as she pitched on top of another wave. Water flooded over the tubes and all around my feet. I snatched at the charm. It wouldn't come away because it had become tangled around the anchor warp. I yanked again, but still it wouldn't break. I was becoming annoyed. So, summoning every bit of strength left after two nights without sleep, I grabbed it and pulled.

It finally came free, and I hurled it into the waves.

On reaching Charlie again, I felt a surge of relief. I again took the helm and waited . . . waited for the miracle of calm seas. But the sea never even looked like subsiding. It stayed just as rough through both our shifts, and I was tiring.

This vast ocean just didn't care about us, didn't care if we reached Greenland or not, if we capsized and drowned. It was so immense, and we were so very small. This can be the sea's greatest quality – the way it reminds us of our own mortality. But that reminder is also very humbling. Being big or brave doesn't seem to count for much. In fact, even just trying your best and slogging your guts out means very little. It is irrelevant, and only the sea decides who wins the battle.

All we could do was endure. Waiting, like ants on a motorway.

Once again, as shadows of exasperation closed in, I reached for the Dictaphone's pouch and pressed record . . .

I am getting exhausted. The other guys are as well. They are doing so well, trying to knuckle through this thing, but it has been exhausting. I just want to get to Greenland. I am going to sleep, and I'm not going to move for six months. I don't care. I'm not going on another adventure like this. It's too intense, too exhausting. It's so different from climbing Everest: there we had that stillness, and you could always climb into a tent and get away. But this is so relentless – the pounding and the wet. There is no escape. I just long for it to be calm.

This is an endurance exercise, and it gets much more frightening at night, because you just can't see the waves. All you see is the white water.

We're still going at 8 knots, not much faster than running pace. But the guys have been incredible. I feel so genuinely proud of them right now. I thought the people without military backgrounds would be struggling, but Nige and Charlie have been an inspiration.

Charlie happened to be helming when I climbed along to the foredeck. My whole life was in his hands, and he held everything together. Not long ago, he was asking for advice, but now he has mastered the helm, he's in control, and I trust him completely. That's very special.

Nige is coping amazingly, considering. He's wet through and should be bloody miserable, but he just turned to me to say he could murder a Danish pastry and a cappuccino. He smiled faintly. But Nige's great quality is that he just gets on with things. It's these small things that make such a huge difference.

So much can go wrong on this boat: if the engine stops, we're in big trouble; if the forecast is wrong, we're in big trouble; if the navigation is not done properly, we're lost. But each of these guys has taken responsibility for his job, and everyone trusts that person to do it. Not just with words but with their life.

Things are really bad right now, but there's something pretty unique about this situation: five men in a small boat, all trusting one another, looking after one another. Caring.

I had told everyone so often that there would be times when we would be at our wits' ends, but also that it is in those times that I need them to give that little bit extra. To laugh, to watch out for someone as they pee, to dig out a chocolate bar for the guy on watch, when you're exhausted. This is what really matters, and they have all done this over and over again.

These four guys are just bloody brilliant British people. They show so much quiet, cheerful strength, and yet I know how cold and wet they are because I can feel them shivering alongside me. I will buy the biggest round ever if we reach Greenland, I promise.

When I finished recording these thoughts, it took me some time to push the stop button on the Dictaphone. It should have been the simplest task, but my fingers were numb, and I fumbled around angrily for several minutes.

By midnight, three o'clock in the morning back home, I decided to call Chloë again, to keep her informed of our progress and to check that the Danish navy had been alerted to our situation.

I got through second go this time and told her our status.

'And one other thing,' I added.

'Yes?' she said.

'Can you call Charlie Mackesy and ask him to pray for us? He'll understand, even if it is three in the morning. I really need his help.'

Charlie was my best man at our wedding and one of my closest friends. An artist in London, he is also Jesse's godfather, and in this desperate situation I needed to feel that he was praying for us, praying that everything would somehow be all right.

Charlie recalls:

I was staying with my sister in Yorkshire, fast asleep when the mobile rang under my pillow. I woke up, looked at the display, saw it was Chloë and immediately knew Bear was either in real trouble or was dead. It would have to be something terrible for her to call me at three o'clock in the morning.

She told me Bear wanted me to pray for him because he was stuck in this storm. It was getting worse, there were icebergs about and he didn't think he was going to get out of it.

To be honest, I wasn't feeling very full of any sort of faith at the time, but I went downstairs, sat quietly in a chair and said a prayer. I simply asked God to calm the storm. I slowly became aware of a strange, but very clear image, where it was pitch black, ice was everywhere and people were screaming. I prayed for it to go quiet, and then fell asleep in the chair. I woke up in the early hours of the morning with a sense of calm, and went back upstairs to bed with no idea what had happened.

Meanwhile, three of us were soon back in the sardine tin, once again trying to ignore the stinging, salty spray and the relentless battering of being lifted up and then thumped down. I was done in. I lay there, wedged against Nige and Mick, and out of sheer exhaustion I somehow fell asleep. It was a magic relief from the grim reality of our slow-burning failure.

I woke with a start. It was just after 5.30 a.m., and immediately I became aware that something was different. The boat was planing. We were surging forward smoothly and the sea was millpond-calm. I blinked hard, suspended in that demi-world between sleep and being awake. I blinked again.

This was for real.

Andy and Charlie were helming, and chatting. Then Andy turned towards me and smiled.

'Things are starting to look up, Bear,' he said. 'We're doing twenty-two knots.'

I sat up and looked around. I couldn't believe my eyes. The sea had just died away. The apparently endless storm had ended. The sky was clear blue. It was a beautiful day. I sat and stared.

'We've got about 400 litres in the centre line tank,' Andy continued. 'I think we might just do it.'

He grinned at me.

Elated, I began to get up from the sardine tin. For the first time, we had a real chance of making it.

I knew we should call the base team in London, just to let them know our situation had improved, and I duly phoned Chloë. She in turn contacted Shara to say everything was all right; Shara then phoned Charlie Mackesy in Yorkshire, just to let him know all was well and that his prayers had been answered. Charlie suddenly adopted this guru-like status. It was very funny. But God had shone on us very clearly and I was in no doubt of that at all.

We were not quite out of trouble but we were all beginning to believe we could make it to Greenland. Everybody was wide awake, enjoying the sunshine and our newfound speed. Andy was carefully monitoring the fuel situation, with Charlie helping him read the dials. Mick's lifejacket had also gone off sometime during the last twenty-four hours, and he and Nige were laughing at themselves, looking like drowned rats dressed in bright yellow blow-up jackets. It was our finest time on the entire expedition so far. We forgot the wet, the cold and the hunger and enjoyed being able to talk for the first time in days. The wind had disappeared and the boat was flying.

At last, at 9 a.m., Greenland appeared on the horizon.

We were still 65 nautical miles offshore, but even from that distance we could identify the gigantic mountains and broken glaciers of this, the largest and most remote island on the planet.

'How are we doing on fuel, Andy?'

He looked up from the console. 'I'm trying to drain all the different tanks into one. It's hard to tell exactly but we're still going, eh?'

The sea was like glass, and there was a crisp chill in the air. I had never before seen sea like glass at that distance offshore. It was incredible, and I felt the mercy of God that morning. We were exhausted, but we were so relieved.

Seagulls were swooping above us, playful puffins fluttered frantically in front of our bow, and stunning-shaped icebergs were dotted along the coastline as far as we could see. The miles were dropping off behind us fast. It was a dream.

We eventually eased carefully past a cluster of giant growler icebergs that surrounded the small harbour of Nanortalik. They floated freely, sculpted like vast statues, and you could see their huge mass of cobalt blue ice under the surface of the calm water. We had finally reached Greenland.

We were met at the small harbour pier by the mayor and a group of locals. They held out strong hands to help us ashore. I had never felt so pleased to arrive anywhere.

Andy took a look at the last tank.

'How much fuel is left?'

'About fifty litres, I reckon,' Andy replied.

Fifty litres? That was perhaps enough to have kept us going for another half-hour on the ocean. We had started the leg with 4,000 litres. Fifty? It was the tightest of margins. It was nothing. Bluntly put, if that storm had raged for thirty minutes longer, we would not have made it. It had been that close.

We had been lucky, very lucky. I knew that, and I was with four men who were deeply grateful to reach dry land.

We all were desperate to lie down and sleep, but first there were a couple of SAT phone calls to be made.

I called Chloë to tell her the good news that we had finally arrived in Nanortalik; then I called Captain Pennefather direct.

'What was your fuel state when you arrived?' he asked.

'Vapour,' I replied, smiling.

Above. Our first iceberg. To give some perspective, this one is over eight miles away

Right. Arnold & Son Explorer in the Greenland fjords

Leaving Nanortalik, following the ice towards the mouth of
the Prince Christiansen Sound

Nige taking time out to write his diary midway through
the Prince Christiansen Sound

Above. Repacking and stowing kit in the Prince Christiansen Sound

Right. Trying to catch up with some precious sleep as we leave the coast of Greenland. We are sleeping in the bows to try and bring the weight forward to increase our speed

The sun sets over the ice plateaux of Greenland behind us

Entering the big head seas. We knuckle down as the conditions dramatically deteriorate. The barometer plummets some 400 miles from Iceland. In the worst conditions, taking photos became impossible

Dawn finally arrives after a night of terrifying storms off Iceland

Andy stares out longingly towards Iceland, only fifteen miles away but
still hidden, at the end of our frightening ordeal

One of the rare clear sunsets captured as we leave the Vestmann Islands

Against the backdrop of the remote, northern coast of Scotland,
the *Arnold & Son Explorer* completes its journey. *(Kinloch)*

Above. We finally hit land!
The homecoming on the beach
of a small cove at Kinloch,
north Scotland

Right. Nige's face says it all.
Scotland at last! *(Kinloch)*

Below. Lt Andy Leivers and
Bear Grylls, holding the Royal Navy's
White Ensign aloft as they arrive
in John O'Groats.
(David Cheskin / PA Photos)

The moment we had all been longing for: celebrating the 'Mumm' way in Scotland! *(David Cheskin / PA Photos)*

Holding my little son Jesse the day I returned. His look says: 'Dad, take a bath'

9. GOOD NEWS, BAD NEWS

Indecision is the thief of opportunity.

Napoleon Bonaparte

Sleeping for a couple of hours, taking a hot shower, getting something decent to eat: these are the kinds of thing most of us take for granted every day of our lives. After 700 miles of living in an open boat on the Labrador Sea, exhausted and salt-burnt, these simple acts took on a meaning that is hard to describe.

The Inuit mayor showed us to our 'hotel', which was a relatively large corrugated building surrounded by several rows of smaller corrugated houses. But at that moment, a five-star West End hotel could not have been more enticing.

We hung our soaking kit up to dry in the dusty boiler room, and Nige, Mick and I were asleep, fully clothed, before we had even closed the door of our small bedroom. The shower could wait a few minutes longer.

We woke an hour or so later; it was mid-afternoon. Andy and Charlie were beginning to let their hair down and have a few beers with some of the locals. They had certainly earned a night off.

There was an Internet terminal in the hotel reception and I stayed behind with Mick to check the weather forecast on the increasingly familiar series of websites.

Our next leg was going to be the longest of the expedition, and probably the most challenging: just over 800 miles round

Greenland, across the Denmark Strait and on to Reykjavik in Iceland. The web pages took a while to download, and I watched them slowly unfold on the screen.

My heart sank as I read what appeared.

'There will be a Force Three weather pattern for the next forty-eight hours ... and severe storms are expected to arrive in the Denmark Strait by Friday afternoon.'

It was already Tuesday evening.

There was no problem with a Force Three weather pattern. That would be ideal. That was about as good as the weather was ever going to get in this part of the world. The real problem was that, for the second time on the expedition, just like in St Mary's, I was being presented with a dangerous dilemma, a fifty–fifty decision, a roll of the dice.

The choice was straightforward: either we seized the latter part of the forty-eight-hour weather window, banking on reaching Iceland before the main storms hit this far north, or we played safe and waited in Nanortalik until conditions improved.

Was forty-eight hours long enough to reach Iceland? Maybe it was just, if we left now, but that was impossible. We couldn't even refuel until 10 a.m. the following day. That reduced the forty-eight-hour window to thirty-six hours. But what was the alternative? A wait that might not break until the ice-packs returned in earnest?

Yet again, I felt as though I was being challenged to gamble with our lives. And I hate gambling. It just takes one bad call to make it your last. Mick looked at me. Only a matter of hours ago we had been pleading for land, dreaming of respite from the fury of the sea, and here we were debating whether we should put ourselves back into that furnace. It didn't sit easy at all.

I leaned back in the chair and wished I could be in a situation where the forecast meant the decision was obvious, either way.

Mick wrote all the data down, to spell it out clearly.

The advantages of staying were that we would all get the few days of rest that we so desperately needed after our ordeal in the Labrador Sea. The drawback was that the bad weather could remain in place for three to four weeks by the look of the weather patterns moving up from the south. That would mean we could be stuck in Greenland until September when winter would begin to draw in again. The temperatures then drop even further, the ice starts to compact, and it would become impossible to complete the expedition.

'Who dares wins,' rolls off the tongue so easily. It is much harder to say when your life is in that dare.

No doubt the benefit of leaving Greenland as soon as possible, most probably the following morning, was that we would sustain the momentum of the expedition and, with a bit of luck, reach Iceland before the predicted lows and rough weather really took hold. The danger was if these lows came early; no one wanted to find themselves in another, bigger storm.

An additional factor was that this time we would be racing towards the bad weather, trying to beat it to Iceland. On the

Labrador we had been travelling through the storm, eventually away from trouble. Now the front would be blowing into us, so if we hit it, there would be no respite until port. The longer we took, the worse it would get. We knew that.

The others were now well into the drinking. I could hear them next door in the bar. The tension of the Labrador was getting drowned away in time-honoured fashion.

The little voice at the back of my head was urging me not to be impatient, to be responsible and cautious. I didn't mind waiting, I had always wanted to have some time in this remote, beautiful part of the world, but we had a goal in mind, and instinct told me we had to seize this window of opportunity.

Once again, five lives seemed to rest in my hands. Why couldn't this decision be simple? Mick presented me with the facts in black and white, on paper, in his scrawl that I knew so well. Mike Town concurred. It was my call. But I couldn't make it.

This was a massive decision, and I didn't feel able to make it alone. In search of calm, wise advice, I called Captain Pennefather. He listened quietly as I explained the situation, sketching out the pros and cons.

Willie didn't say much because he didn't need to. He just let me talk through the situation and, as I talked, I gradually began to realize there was really no choice at all. Yes, it was exhausting, it was too soon in an ideal world, and it was maybe a shade risky, but if we were going to complete the expedition, we basically had little choice.

Willie simply, cleverly, gave me the space to reach my own conclusion.

We rang Mike Town once more. Again he confirmed that two big fronts were on their way from the south and that if we didn't leave soon, we would probably have to remain in Greenland for several weeks. Mick looked once more at the charts, estimating wave heights and our chances of reaching Iceland in the time that this weather window seemed to allow us.

I asked Mick for his honest view on what we should do, no holds barred. I knew it was important to be decisive with the other guys, but Mick was different; he was my closest mate. I could share everything with him, without shame, my real fears and doubts, the sheer uncertainty of it all. I looked at him. His eyes looked tired. Tired of the salt water and now tired of the computer screen.

'So?'

He frowned, paused, then said quietly, 'Bear, I guess we've got to leave in the morning.' He continued, 'Every minute will count. How early do you think we will be able to get away?'

'Well, if we refuel on time, we should be able to leave at around eleven thirty, at a push.'

This didn't even give us time to dry our clothes.

'Instinct is the nose of the mind ... trust it.' This was one of the quotes that we had laminated and stuck on the boat. 'Bloody quotes,' I swore. But it was our answer.

Now I had to break the news to the others.

As I stood outside the bar, grey clouds of doubt scudded in all over again. Was I putting my ambition to complete this expedition ahead of our lives? Was I being impulsive and foolish?

I knew that 80 per cent of the time people die on high mountains because they push on when common sense says they should turn back. Was I doing just that? We had been let off the hook on the Labrador Sea. How smart was it to go straight back out, into possibly even worse weather? But how would we know if we never even tried?

I called them together in a room alongside the bar. They were enjoying a few beers and were not really in the mood for a meeting. I would have felt exactly the same in their position. I felt a strange pang of envy. I didn't want this burden.

'Well, there is good news and bad news,' I began, realizing that none of them was expecting what they were about to hear. 'The good news is that we have a window of good weather, and the bad news is that, to take this opportunity, we must leave as soon as possible in the morning.'

They stood motionless. Nobody said a word.

'It will mean we need to get up at five,' I continued, filling the void, 'and start prepping the boat. It's not great, but it seems our only choice if we are ever to reach Iceland.'

I paused.

'And I'm really sorry we can't delay the weather.'

Mick, at least, had been prepared. Andy, Nige and Charlie just looked understandably fed up. The long-awaited period of rest and recovery after the Labrador crossing was being cancelled. This, I am certain, was the single most difficult moment of the entire expedition.

Mick outlined the reasons for the decision, explaining the weather forecast and how forty-eight, possibly seventy-two, hours of clear weather would be followed by weeks of storms, but Andy was clearly hesitant and uncomfortable.

'Bear, the one thing we all said when we arrived here was that, above all, we didn't want to get caught in bad weather again,' he reminded us. 'We were bloody lucky out there this time. Now you're telling us to go back into it with a shit forecast, with little chance of beating that weather to Iceland. What happens if the fronts come sooner rather than later?'

'I know that's the risk. I don't have an answer for that,' I replied. 'I only have the facts. Study the charts Mick's done and see what you reckon. If we don't all agree, we don't go.'

This took Andy a few minutes to digest. And part of me, if I am honest, longed for someone to say no. The idea of another storm terrified me. Anyone who thinks these expeditions are romantic should have felt the tension in that room. It was palpable. These decisions were critical. My hands were sweating.

'Let's try and get a few hours' sleep now,' I said.

The guys had arrived in high spirits; they returned to their rooms in silence. I was knackered, in mind and body, and as I fell into bed and gazed at the white patterned ceiling, I just hoped we had made the correct decision.

Charlie recalls:

Bear's announcement was a shock, and we did question it, but not in a negative way. In the end, we understood and accepted his logic, and the team ethic came through. Such team spirit was new for me.

By nature, I have tended to be a loner, working as a freelance cameraman and often travelling on my own. I live my own life, and I have always been happy with that. However, on this small boat, being part of the team was everything, relying on other people and knowing that they relied on me. It felt good.

So, when Bear said he wanted to leave in the morning, we didn't just accept it without question. This wasn't the army. We studied the data and discussed the issues, but, in the end, we agreed and moved forward together. That was it. Whatever happened after that, there would be no recriminations.

Nige recalls:

It wasn't a great moment when Mick and Bear said we would have to leave, and it wasn't too great when, the next morning, I discovered that my boots were still sodden wet. It was not ideal that I had to start the leg by putting soaking wet boots on; but I guess the weather didn't give us much choice.

There are not many situations that don't look better after a decent night's sleep, and when we all woke at 5.30, everyone appeared more cheerful and purposeful. Everyone now accepted the logic. We had agreed on the decision together, and the team was moving forward as one. Nobody was on the touchlines. We were all players and had made our own calls.

Mick and Andy started preparing the boat, which still looked a mess after the Labrador crossing; Charlie and Nige were doing their best to dry and repack all the equipment, and I settled the hotel bill, arranged the refuelling and sorted out the customs forms. With luck, I reckoned, we would be able to get away before noon.

We all knew the blue sky above us would not last for ever and the forty-eight-hour clock was ticking.

The mayor had invited us to lunch, but I dropped by his home to say this was no longer possible. I explained that every minute counted in our race to cross the Denmark Strait and reach Iceland before the storms arrived. He understood completely.

It was almost half past eleven when I reached the quayside. The guys had done a fantastic job, and we were almost ready to leave.

Alex Rayner, our PR man in London, had been asking us repeatedly to do a select few radio interviews. I knew that I should do these, but I felt uncomfortable. This just wasn't the right time. I reneged on my promise to Alex, turned off the SAT phone, and quietly hoped he would understand.

However, a minute later, a radio station got through on Nige's mobile phone. It was BBC Radio Five Live.

'Bear, we'll call you back in twenty minutes for a live slot,' said the producer in London. 'Is that OK?'

The guys were waiting in the boat. We were refuelled and ready to go. They had met our deadline exactly. It was 11.30 a.m. precisely. They all looked at me.

I put the phone to my ear again. 'I'm really sorry, but we just don't have the time.'

'Just twenty minutes?'

'Not this time; we have to leave now. I'm really sorry.'

They were clearly a bit put out, but away in their London studio they were not to know that for us to wait another twenty minutes could turn out to be the difference between reaching Iceland safely and getting trapped in the oncoming gales.

We didn't have that sort of time to waste. I jumped aboard the boat and Andy turned the key once more. If all went to plan, this engine would run continuously until we reached Iceland. And that was a long way from here. Iceland, in my little son Jesse's *Children's Atlas of the World*, was still one whole page away.

The first ten hours of this leg unfolded as one of those experiences that will remain with me for ever. It was a privilege to behold.

Our route took us down the south-west coast of Greenland and then through the Prince Christiansen Sound, effectively cutting off the southern cape of Greenland and bringing us out on the eastern side. The natural features of Prince Christiansen Sound are some of the most remote and unsung beauties of the world. Maybe this is what makes them so magical. They are so rarely seen.

I can only think of one word to describe our reaction as we began to weave our way through the sheer fjords in front of us: stunned.

Sheer, vertical walls of rock, at least 2,000 feet high, rose straight out of the water into giant, snow-capped, jagged peaks. The depth of this fjord was such that it went off the scale of our instruments. Several times, we took the boat up to the rock face, stared upwards, and marvelled at these natural skyscrapers.

This was a living, changing landscape. Glaciers tumbled down thousands of feet into the still, icy water. I had seen icefalls on Everest, where the frozen ice ruptures and breaks its way dramatically down cliff faces. But here, the glacier crashed directly into the fjord.

Thousands of pieces of ice, ranging from small lumps to enormous bergs, were floating in the water, and it was exhilarating to see and feel the ice knocking against the aluminium hull, as we wove our way through the bergs. The *Arnold and Son Explorer* had been designed for these conditions, and it eased its way elegantly through the Sound.

Twice, the black mass of a whale appeared, suddenly rising out of the water within 50 yards of the boat and then disappearing with a casual swish of its 6-foot tail. It was unbelievable to sit and watch.

We passed through this wonderland in awe. The sun was bright in the midday sky, without a cloud in sight, and we were dressed in light clothes and fleeces. For the only time on the entire expedition we let the rota slip, each of us simply took turns in helming, while the rest sprawled out on the foredeck, writing diaries, listening to their Walkmans or just basking in the wonder of this place. It was a special time and for once we could recoup a bit of energy. We would need it.

Not another person for miles around; just us, in this frozen paradise.

Charlie recalls:

The icebergs were colossal, coming in all sorts of weird shapes and sizes. Some had these strange kinds of spires and they genuinely resembled cathedrals. They were certainly that big. They had a translucent tinge, and many had these incredible cracks of bright blue running through them. They were astonishing.

We saw a variety of whales – Humpback, Minke – but none came much closer than 50 metres, probably because our jet drive was making such a racket, and that meant that, unfortunately, despite all the sightings, I never got my 'Attenborough' shot on camera!

We all felt a sense of peace, a quiet contentment. It was the moment I had hungered for so much. It was just nature and my friends. Pure magic.

These beautiful, isolated places, where just one hidden rockface, high above a glistening glacier, stands out so proud and majestic, feed a man's soul. They are untouched by human contact, like a tiny flower in a dense jungle that serves no purpose for mankind – a flower that will remain unseen for ever. To me, such places are simply God's extravagance.

We had come to this place, far from civilization and completely uninhabited, and we found glaciers, mountains and icebergs that were truly exquisite. But we knew it couldn't last for ever, and all of us dreaded the next bend in the fjord being the last.

Eventually we turned the final corner of the Sound and were confronted by 20 miles of fjord leading straight to the ocean. This spectacular stretch of water was bordered on either side by even larger mountains, which would part every once in a while to afford a glimpse of the snow-capped plateaux of Greenland behind.

But our gaze was fixed on what lay ahead of us in the open seas, and for the first time that day we could feel the cold Arctic wind on our faces. This wind was being funnelled down the fjord but it was nothing violent, just a stiff, steady breeze, almost like a warning. It was announcing the ocean ahead. And it was beckoning us forward.

Each of us put on extra fleeces and began to clamber into our survival suits. We made certain everything was correctly stowed and the boat properly organized. We had learnt a lot from the Labrador: about rough-water stowing of food and supplies, about waterproofing kit effectively, about wearing the right amount of layers. In some ways, we had been caught out by that storm, and we didn't want to make the same mistakes again. Everyone could feel the stakes were rising.

Before long we were dressed in our full gear – balaclavas, helmets, inner and outer gloves, two pairs of thermal socks, five layers of clothing under the dry-suits, the lot – and a quietness, a tension descended on the boat. It was 7.20 p.m. We could hardly move now, we were so bulked up. But experience had taught us to be ready. We sat in silence. The mouth of the fjord was still flat calm, with only the ripples of the funnelled wind bristling on the water.

'OK, Nige, how far to Iceland?' I asked.

'In a straight line, 630 nautical miles,' he replied.

'All right then, with a bit of luck we should reach Reykja-vik by 15.30 hrs the day after tomorrow.'

As we reached the edge of the fjord, where the Sound runs into the wide open ocean and the Denmark Strait, we stopped one last time. The boat idled lazily, dwarfed by the glaciers and cliffs on either side of us. We had one last SAT phone call to make.

Mike Town was waiting for us to call. He checked the weather forecast again. It was still clear for the next thirty-six hours, with Force Fives or Sixes coming up towards Iceland after that. If we could be within reach of Iceland by that time, we could manage these winds for the last stage into port. That was good enough for us. Now we just had one last box to tick before we set out to sea.

Tucked into the edge of the cliffs, at the mouth of the Sound, is one of the remotest weather stations in this part of the world. The scientists there are more familiar than anyone with these waters, and they understand how unpredictable they can be. Their advice would be invaluable.

We saw their aerials and a cluster of huts from a few miles down the Sound, and we managed to get them on the radio.

'Hi. Where are you heading?' they asked.

'To Iceland,' I replied.

There was a pause.

'What's the weather looking like?' I continued. I didn't want to put words in their mouths.

'Well, it looks good for twenty-four hours, then it *should* be OK for another twelve hours after that; then it's deteriorating towards Iceland. It depends on how fast that low pressure sweeps north. But I reckon you should be OK. Wouldn't you like a cup of tea and something to eat before you leave?'

'Thanks,' I said, 'but we're all dressed up like astronauts and ready to go. We really ought to keep moving.'

We thanked them and signed off.

The forecasts sounded consistent with what we had had from the UK, but I also knew we were moving into some of the most uncharted waters on the planet. The US military had only recently put weather buoys in place to measure the wave heights. They had no need for such data previously.

We had taken good advice, we knew the facts and we were going for it. I packed the SAT phone away in its watertight pouch in the console and crawled back out.

We were still drifting around slowly, weaving among a small cluster of icebergs in the last little inlet before the ocean. It was as if these small bergs were wary of moving into the open seas. To be honest, I felt a little bit the same.

We eased the throttle open, turned the boat's nose from land and headed out into the Denmark Strait between Greenland and Iceland, and almost 700 miles of open sea.

In all my research, I hadn't found much about this part of the route. What I did discover in one geographical document was pretty blunt: 'The Denmark Strait is one of the most difficult of large ocean straits in which to carry out any sort of research. Inhospitable weather and the frequent presence of ice make ship operation severely difficult. Try somewhere warmer.'

This wasn't quite what I was looking for.

As we headed away from the ice plateaux of the Greenland coastline, the sea was glassy-calm before us. Not even a ripple of wind now anywhere.

'It's like the *Marie Céleste*,' Nige said.

He was right.

We had reached the ocean to find, not the severe conditions that we had feared, but an eerie stillness. Dusk was falling, the sea was like a mirror, and a dense fog was descending. Before long it had completely obscured Greenland from sight.

I knew what Nige meant. It did feel as though we had been transported to the *Marie Céleste*, the fabled ship that was found drifting on the ocean, untouched and unmanned.

A flock of puffins were floundering around in the water, and as we headed towards them they flapped awkwardly as they tried to take off. How the hell did such small, clumsy birds survive the storms these waters must see? I had no idea. They looked so fragile and out of place. But they did, and it was spectacular and humbling to watch these wonders of nature fussing all around us.

We were managing a speed of only 13 knots because the boat was still so heavy with fuel at the start of such a long leg, but the rocking motion of the gently rolling waves was ideal for sleep. As we maintained the rota, each of us managed to get some rest during our hours in the sardine tin.

It was a glorious night and I remember waking apprehensively, opening my eyes and half expecting to find the sea churning and throwing the boat around, but it wasn't. It was still calm.

However, I still felt very nervous. I wasn't sure why.

I knew that every hour that passed was an hour nearer Iceland, but I longed to go faster, to get more miles under our belt while the weather was so good.

'How are we doing?' I asked Mick.

'Yeah, it looks OK,' he replied. 'We've done 205 miles since we left.'

I looked around the boat. Everything was neat and ready, and everyone was resting.

The dawn felt a little cooler, but that was to be expected; we were heading in a north-easterly direction all the time, towards a latitude of 64 degrees north. It was still calm as we ploughed on through the gentle rollers.

A few hours later, Charlie and I were sitting together at the console when, out of nowhere, we were confronted by a cruise ship ahead on the horizon. It had been a real surprise to me that we had seen so little other shipping on the expedition so far. I had expected to see much more. The truth was that this was the first ship we had seen in almost 2,000 miles. We were so excited. I tried to raise the captain on the radio, to get some further info on the weather conditions ahead (even though there wasn't much we would have been able to do about it out here).

We couldn't see the name of the vessel. So we tried this instead:

'Hello, big ship, this is little yellow boat.'

A Danish voice replied, 'Hello, how are you?'

'Fine,' I responded. 'Just fine.'

He said he had heard about our expedition, and he wished us luck. I detected an element of foreboding in his voice when he said that the 'fair weather had lasted well in the Denmark Strait'. He asked if there was much ice around the southern edges of Greenland, where he was heading, and we told him it was broken up and passable.

As he spoke, a cluster of people appeared on the deck of the cruise ship. They were all peering down on the small yellow boat passing in the shadow of their ship. We just sat there, feeling a bit ridiculous and very small, imagining what they were thinking.

'Oh well,' said Mick, waving from the sardine tin, 'at least the captain won't be getting too many complaints from his passengers about the state of their cabins. I think we have given them a new perspective on the words "living quarters".'

It was nearly midday on Thursday, our second day at sea after leaving Greenland, conditions were still good and we were making reasonable progress. If our weather forecasts were right, there was almost another twenty-four hours in our window of decent weather, and that should be enough time to get us within reach of Iceland. All seemed well and we had no reason to imagine that anything would change.

We noticed the wind freshen into the afternoon. It was not dramatic, but it was marked. Where we had been expecting Force Four, we were moving into Force Five winds.

But that was OK, I told myself. The bad weather was still 1,000 miles to our south.

Or it was supposed to be.

By evening, the sea was building and the spray had returned, every thirty seconds or so, cold and uncomfortable, and I started to notice the movement of the boat becoming more pronounced. She was taking these head-on waves well, digging the deep-V hull into the water as it rose to meet her bows.

It wasn't too bad.

'It's OK, isn't it?' I said to Nige that second evening.

'Yep, this is nothing like the Labrador,' he replied.

'No,' I said. 'No dramas.'

Three hours later, I happened to glance over at Nige. It was our habit to keep a vague look out for each other. I looked again. He was staring intently at his watch. I knew what he was staring at. His barometer.

A barometer simply measures the air pressure, but it is still, in this modern age of electronics, the most accurate and reliable indicator of any bad weather ahead. It had read 1,026 millibars when we left Greenland and had remained pretty much unchanged ever since.

But something had obviously changed now. Nige looked blank and frightened.

I was watching him.

'What's it say?' I asked.

'It dropped to 996 millibars,' he replied. 'That's impossible. I have never seen anything like this before.'

The barometer had dropped 30 millibars. Much later, Mike Town would say this was almost a meteorological impossibility – it was too steep. But it happened. We all saw it.

Our weather window had slammed shut. The night was just beginning and we didn't know what the hell we were going into.

Three hundred miles out to sea, almost exactly midway between Greenland and Iceland, there was no longer any-where to hide.

Our ordeal would soon begin.

10. TERROR

When you are going through hell, keep walking.

Sir Winston Churchill

Our hopes plunged with the barometer.

All of us knew we had been racing against the weather. But now we were racing *into* that weather. There would be no respite until we reached Iceland, and we knew we were in difficulty.

We had been told the weather window would last forty-eight hours, but the low pressure had moved north at an alarming speed. That precious window had lasted only thirty hours.

The rota meant it was my turn to rest in the sardine tin, and I desperately went over the situation in my head. Clear, logical thought was hard. 'How did this happen? Was this my fault? Should we, after all, have stayed longer in Greenland?'

In confusion, I reached for the Dictaphone.

We're back in the really big seas now. Waves are crashing over the boat again, and we're all getting soaked. Our kit that we had laid out so carefully on the tubes to dry whilst in the Sound is now getting drenched once more.

Our bodies are being slammed around the boat, and it's just relentless. When you're not on watch, sitting at the console, you have to brace yourself in your seat, tensing your stomach muscles, over and over again. The boat seems to get picked up every thirty seconds or so. If it lands on the keel, it's OK. If it lands on its side, it sounds as if the boat is breaking apart under us.

I am dehydrated, but I can't get across the boat to get a drink. Moving around is so hard. I've got a really bad headache from the slamming, and each wave makes me wince. It's impossible to have a pee: I tried clinging to the console, but you need both hands to undo your fly-zip. In the end, I just gave up. There's no chance of getting a drink, eating or having a pee so long as these conditions continue. We just cling on for all we're worth.

We're 325 miles off Iceland. That's still a hell of a long way, when we can hardly make nine knots; and this storm is getting worse; that is what frightens me the most.

Twenty-five-foot waves were rolling, breaking and crashing all around us. And from the level of a small, open RIB, they felt immense and terrifying.

The water pouring over us, hour after hour, was icy. We were now just south of the Arctic Circle, in seas that were freezing enough to sustain tens of thousands of icebergs. This wet cold was terrible. Our underclothes inevitably, over time, got damp because the seams began to let in small amounts of water, and slowly all this then seeped down our arms and chests. Every part of our bodies felt drenched, but it was the wind that really made us cold.

This wind whipped over the console and chilled every exposed part of us; every gust carried with it more of the freezing sea spray. Heading *into* this wind made it twice as strong. It was both the storm and our forward speed combined. Wherever we sat or curled up, there was nowhere to hide from it. All we could do was hug one another in the sardine tin, pull the tarpaulin up to our waists and try to get through the next hour.

In these conditions, our salvation was the kit we wore. From the very first night on the Labrador Sea, when it had got so cold that we had had to stop the boat and put on extra layers, we had learned the hard way how to try to keep as warm as possible. Our survival depended on it.

From the inside out, the full kit was an unbelievable amount: next to the skin, we wore a thick, fleecy long-sleeved top and thick thermal long-john trousers; then a heavy-duty fleece, then Gortex salopettes and a Gortex fleece jacket; on top of all this went an all-in-one survival dry-suit, and another windproof and waterproof ocean jacket on top of that.

On our hands we had inner fleece gloves inside big waterproof mittens. We also had sealed fleece diving gloves, but both sets inevitably ended up sodden. You just interchanged in a futile attempt to warm your fingers.

On our heads we had fleece balaclavas and a Gortex balaclava over that; on top of these we wore RNLI Gecko helmets. But even these couldn't keep the water out. It got in everywhere: our hair was soaked and our faces and necks had water constantly dripping down them.

Most of this kit was provided by Musto, and I will never forget standing in Musto's headquarters, in Basildon, a year earlier. It was a swelteringly hot summer's day, and Keith Musto, the founder of the clothing company, was helping me try all this on. Within minutes, I was sweating. Keith found it very amusing, me standing in the stock room like a giant Mr Blobby, dreading it as he approached me to add yet another layer.

'You will need it all,' he added, as he tugged me into another fleece. 'This kit will keep you alive. It's the best in the world. But have no doubt about it, if it gets really bad out there, whatever you are wearing, you will still be cold.'

I truly could never have then imagined any conditions being cold enough to make me shiver with all this amount of fleece and Gortex kit on. I could hardly move. But then I had never been in this sort of wet wind chill, this far north, so exposed, for so long before. Here in this tiny corner of the vast, 41-million-square-mile ocean, curled in a ball on the floor of this small, open boat, I found myself shivering uncontrollably.

The key to coping with cold is not to allow yourself to get to the stage of being really cold. That might sound obvious, but I have learned from climbing that if you allow yourself to get that cold, it's almost too late to do anything about it. It's much harder to get warm again. But here there was nothing we could do: we had no shelter in which to hide from the wind and rain and spray, and we had nothing more we could wear. All we had was what we stood in.

We relied entirely on one another to keep an eye out for signs of hypothermia, to be constantly aware of the tell-tale signs of extreme cold – shaking hands, slow reactions and sluggish responses – and to help anyone who seemed in trouble. Hypothermia hits silently and often very quickly. The team needed to look after themselves, and everyone needed to be aware of the indicators. If somebody is feeling cold and is crunched up in a ball, trying to protect their core warmth, that's a good sign that they are aware and rational; on the other hand, if they are lying on their back, with their arms at their side, head and body exposed, not caring, then that is not good.

It's good if someone sits up, offers you a Mars bar and shouts, 'Hey, catch'; and it's not good if they don't even have the energy to sit up and get the Mars bars, let alone try to eat one.

We tried to drink something, maybe a cupful of water poured over our face and mouth, every few hours to stay hydrated. I ended up trying to do this once every full rota, i.e. every five hours. It gave me a focus, and I stuck to it. If one of us wasn't drinking, someone needed to notice.

Every little ritual became recognizable and important to us: the way in which each of us sat, or ate, or helmed, or slept. We recognized what was normal for each of us. Any change in the ritual, like any other change in the routine, was often an early sign of something starting to go wrong.

This expedition wasn't about trying to be brave or strong in front of one another, or thinking it was somehow stoic never to admit that you were struggling or something was wrong. It was about being brave enough to say just how you felt, weak or strong; it was about being honest enough to admit occasionally we needed some comfort or a helping hand, being able to say we were frightened. It was about being together, about staying close. All said and done, it was simply about staying alive.

But we were suffering now. We were being lashed by the rain, and our eyes were stinging from the spray. We were getting tired from continually bracing ourselves against the violence of the waves, and our heads were aching from the deafening roar of the engine.

Darkness made things even worse. It became impossible to see the waves, to know where to guide the boat to minimize the slamming. We would stare ahead transfixed, trying desperately to determine the oncoming sea. All we could see of the horizon was a vague line between the pitch black sea and the dark grey, menacing sky. Suddenly, this horizon would disappear and be replaced by a wall of black water, then a final burst of white as the crest of the wave came into view, and then there would be the roar as it crashed over the boat. Those final moments of frothing white water were always the most terrifying, as you braced yourself once more.

You'd cling on to something, anything, and pray.

Often, it seemed the best place to be was sitting in the so-called 'deckchair' on the side of the boat. We had worked out how we could pull a thin plastic storm sheet over us and hide away. If we trapped the bottom of this sheet under our feet and sat on the rest of it, we could just about escape the spray and the wind, and convince ourselves, for a few precious moments, that we were safe. This thin veneer of orange plastic was our comfort blanket, an opportunity to float away into our dreams. For me, they were always dreams of being at home.

It was Charlie's turn in the deckchair now. I was back in the sardine tin, trying to ignore the discomfort. I heard Mick shouting at me, even though his head was only inches from mine.

'This bloody weather – it's not supposed to be here!' he screamed over the noise.

Mick recalls:

I felt this heavy guilt. The weather window had closed much earlier than we expected, and getting the forecast right was my area of responsibility. I started to feel as if the guys were looking at me across the boat and wondering: 'Mick, what's happening?' I felt it was my fault.

Of course it wasn't Mick's fault. It wasn't anybody's fault. The only fair way to judge our decision to leave Greenland is to assess the decision in the circumstances that prevailed at the time. The reality was that in Nanortalik we received advice from three separate sources of information and they all gave us a forty-eight- to seventy-two-hour window. We had had to go. But nobody was to know that this front would arrive sooner than forecast, or that it would be much deeper and more sinister than anticipated.

There were no recriminations. We had to look forward, not back.

As time moved on past eleven o'clock on this second night in the Denmark Strait, six hours into the heavy seas and howling gale, Nige and I found ourselves in the dark, squatting on the floor, trying to hold on while opening the food sack to grab something to eat – anything. Nige pulled out a crushed and split flapjack. The wrapper was broken and it was wet. He steadied himself, broke it in two and handed one half to me. I ate it in one.

'Ooh, I'd love to be in the curry house now,' Nige gushed, 'with Hussein and Mohammed and the trolley, laden with murgs and poppadoms! Absolutely lovely!'

He was smiling at me with relish, and for a moment, a brief moment, we were a million miles away.

It had become almost customary that every Sunday we would all go to the Indian restaurant in our local square. Hussein and Mohammed, the waiters, knew our orders by heart.

'Oh, and don't forget a bit of extra zing in the korma,' I would remind them jokingly, while whistling and twiddling my fingers in imitation of adding a bit of extra chilli. Hussein would laugh, and Shara would roll her eyes; it was always the same old jokes between us. It all felt a long, long way from our small, open boat in this tiny part of the North Atlantic Ocean. But the memory provided us with a fleeting moment of comfort in the nightmare.

Nige looked back at me. He was tired, I could tell. But he still managed a smile.

Charlie was doing OK, but he was also starting to get really cold. One of the first things the army instils in you is the ability to look after yourself when it gets miserable. It is simple self-discipline. Charlie was always a really tough and gritty character, but he didn't have a military background, and his clothing and equipment always seemed to be a bit more chaotic and disorganized than ours. My stuff is always a mess back home, but somehow, when I am away, I become much more careful and neat. I need to know where everything is. It's just habit.

However, as a result, Charlie had to put up with much worse conditions than the rest of us. His spare gloves, for example, were soaking long before ours. He hadn't had them wrapped up well enough in their waterproofing. But he never seemed to grumble. He just got on with it.

For so much of the expedition, Charlie had an almost impossible task. Filming under these conditions was nigh on impossible. Yet despite this, I would often see him fumbling with a radio microphone with cold, shaky fingers, trying to stuff it into its waterproof housing. But no sooner had he taped it to the console or elsewhere, then a wave would tear it loose. Sea-water is a killer to sensitive electronic equipment, and it is a tribute to Charlie that in the early stages of the storm he was filming at all. Despite his best efforts, the bottom line was that, whenever conditions reached gale-force, we were fighting for our lives and neither photography nor filming was possible. The world around us was black and soaking, accompanied by a 120-decibel soundtrack. Not quite ideal lighting or sound conditions.

Still so far from land, our condition was getting serious. We were moving into survival mode. We were nervously fumbling for our harnesses in the dark, feeling them beneath us, concentrating on what we were doing. There was no room for error: fuel readings had to be correct, helming needed to be perfect. One bad reaction could breach the boat in these seas. It was the blackest of nights, and the conditions were still deteriorating.

Things had suddenly got very dangerous very quickly, and it soon became clear that for the second time on the expedition, I would have to call our UK base and alert them to the situation. If conditions continued to plummet at this rate, we would lose all control. Our lives would then rest in the hands of the rescue services, although this far from land, none of us had any idea what sort of rescue could be mounted.

I urged everyone to keep focused as we slowed the boat to a crawl so I could make the call to London.

Once again, in the new, unfamiliar quiet, without the roar of the engine, I knelt down and crawled into the cubbyhole. My hand was shaking now, not just because I was cold but because I was frightened. I patiently waited to get through. It was eight minutes to midnight, their time.

Chloë had just turned out the lights in the hallway of her flat, on her way to bed. She looked at her phone ringing, and her heart sank when she recognized the +88 number identification on the LCD screen and realized this late-night call was coming from the boat. She knew, having been following our tracker, that at this time we were still a long way from Iceland. She realized almost immediately that something was wrong.

'Chloë?'

'Yes, I'm here. What's happening?'

'Get a pen quickly. I need to give you our position.'

I turned to Mick and shouted at him: 'OK, Mick, give me the lat and longs. Loud and clear!'

He yelled at me: 'Six-ah, two-ah, two-ah, seven-ah.'

'Six two, two seven,' I screamed down the receiver, trying to make myself heard above the engine and the storm. 'Did you get that?'

'Yes,' she replied, writing down the numbers on the only piece of paper she could find – a copy of *Time Out*, the London listings magazine.

'Read the numbers back to me, Chloë,' I shouted.

I was cold, wet and exhausted, and I was painfully wedged in this small, dark hole. I needed Chloë to be certain of our precise position so that she could relay this to the rescue services. One number mispronounced or misheard could prove disastrous, even fatal.

'Four-ah, one-ah, three-ah,' Mick shouted in my ear.

'Four one three,' I yelled into the phone. 'So that's six … two … two … seven … four … one … three … North, OK?'

She had the coordinates, and she soon had the latitude reading as well: 31.18.912 West.

'Chloë,' I concluded, 'we're OK, but we're struggling. These seas are much, much bigger than they were on the Labrador. Contact the Icelandic coastguard and give them our position, and keep them posted.'

I turned to Andy, still screaming: 'What's the fuel situation?'

Andy paused, then shouted that the fuel was looking OK; we were still around 250 miles from Reykjavik. I relayed this to Chloë.

I remembered how she had left her safe job at Goldman Sachs for a bit of adventure. Well, now she had it – in spades.

'And please phone Willie as well.'

'OK.'

'We'll phone again in an hour.'

Chloë passed on the message to the rescue services in Reykjavik, as requested, then called Andy Billing, who was awake on our barge in London. She also woke Willie. She would need all the help she could muster.

Chloë recalls:

The call from Bear was brief and troubled; it had come out of the blue. But I had come to expect this. We had agreed before the start of the expedition, when they left England, that Bear would call me at 3 p.m. every day. This never really happened because from the start, even in Halifax, the team were busy at different times with boat preparations, last-minute weather checks and press. It is unfortunately the nature of the beast, and any form of routine was damn near impossible from so far away.

There always seemed so much to do, so many things to sort out, and in the midst of bad weather it seemed impossible to keep track of time. I had promised Chloë I would call again in an hour, so she was sitting up, coffee in hand, waiting for my call. London was in the midst of an uncomfortable heatwave, but it was her concern for us on the ocean, rather than the humidity, that was keeping her wide awake in the early hours of the morning.

In the end, we didn't call until 2.30 a.m., more than an hour and a half late, and Mick spoke to her. I couldn't face the cubbyhole again, I was feeling so seasick. Mick had volunteered instead. He told Chloë the conditions were not improving, but that we were stable and hanging on. We would call again at 8.30 in the morning. Chloë duly passed the news on to Willie. Our base team was all working well, but right now there was nothing they could do to help us. We were going to have to get through this alone.

This night was the time I needed to lead. This was no longer the time to stand back. It was the moment for me to step forward.

Throughout my life, from my army days to the Everest expedition and since, I have never regarded myself as a natural athlete. There have always been people, in all these different fields, who were stronger and fitter than me. But when it comes down to the crunch times, I have always somehow managed to find a little bit extra when it matters most. I've never understood where it comes from.

On Everest, for many weeks early on, I really struggled on the lower sections of the mountain, and there were times when I felt weak and slow, as a climber. But as the months passed and just two of us were finally approaching the summit, I somehow felt my strength return. It shouldn't have been returning then: we hadn't eaten for days, or even peed for over thirty-six hours, our bodies were not functioning and our reserves were gone – we were in the Death Zone and our bodies were physiologically dying, above 26,000 feet. But something was keeping me moving. This strength is not athleticism, it's not fitness; I think it is heart.

And as I clung on in the boat, I felt this was another of those critical moments. It was 1 a.m. and the sea was winning. We were in a crisis, and this was my time to find that heart again.

I didn't want to be impulsive and I didn't want to be cavalier. I was aware that I had to be calm and responsible, and concentrate; I also knew that right now I had to lead. I had been helming for an hour, getting a feel of the conditions, coping, every cell in my body focused, and I knew I shouldn't let go.

'We're stopping the rota,' I shouted. 'I'm going to keep the wheel with Mick for the rest of this night.' The RIB was then hit side-on by a wave that had appeared from nowhere. We all braced against the impact, and then I continued: 'I want you three to get in the sardine tin together and get some rest. I'm going to need your strength for the morning.'

That was my decision. This time, there was no discussion.

I had been as terrified as anyone else as the storm had built up. It was now in full force. We were being pummelled by waves that came at us out of the dark, drenching us, battering us and hitting from all angles. But now, in the heart of this Force Eight gale, hundreds of miles from any land, I felt this strange determination return.

So I kept the helm. I felt emotional and raw, but I was also clear about what Mick and I were doing. Together, the two of us would bring the boat through the storm and through the night. We would keep the boat upright; we would bring it into port. I would need the others to rest and be ready to take over when it was light, but I needed Mick, my oldest friend, to be with me now, beside me.

I didn't want any loose helming during the night as our margin for error had been reduced from maybe 10 per cent to 2 per cent. One mistake, one slip, and the boat could be taken and rolled. You make the right call a thousand times, but just one error of judgement can so often prove fatal. The mountains had shown me that. There was no longer the margin for someone to misjudge a wave or react nervously to a breaking wall of water in front of the bows. The only way I was going to make certain we survived the darkness and the night was by doing the helming myself.

I had pushed everyone to leave Greenland. I had got us all into this hellhole. I would get us through it as well. These were my best friends' lives, and I wouldn't tire now.

Every time we had reached the safety of port before, we had felt as though we had been pardoned. When you walk down a street, it's solid and it doesn't move. There are no surprises. But the ocean is different. It rolls and heaves. It is unpredictable. When you put out to sea – far out to sea, in a small boat – it's like being put out for sacrifice, and ultimately it is the monster of the sea that decides your fate.

That's how I felt. We were being put out for sacrifice, like the heroes in the children's books my mum used to read me when I was young. Waiting to be consumed, devoured, forgotten, never even missed. But I wanted, with every bone in my body, to be home, to hold my wife and son again, and to be safe.

Mick and I would do this together, this one last time.

Mick recalls:

It was the right decision. We were really struggling in the twenty-five-foot waves, and they seemed to be increasing in height and ferocity as the night closed in. Bear and I were just finishing our watch, but Bear had learned how to handle these conditions; he had got the feel of the boat and the sea, and it was just more sensible for the two of us to soldier on through the night than for each guy to come in and start all over again from scratch.

Throughout the previous hour, out of desperation, I had been experimenting with the jet bucket at the stern of the boat. This is a large hood that lowers hydraulically over the jet to give you, effectively, a reverse gear. But we knew that if we lowered it partially over the jet, it would begin to dig the nose of the boat down into the sea slightly. Lowered even further though, it made all the difference, providing stability and grip in the waves. Instead of taking off wildly and slamming off the wave crests, the boat could edge her way over the face of the waves; when the bucket was dipped as she punched through the crest, it pulled the bows sharply down the other side of the wave. Our speed would drop dramatically but it held us more tightly on to the waves' surface.

This all took control though: to feel the different pitch of the bucket and to know at which point to apply it. We were ploughing through the swell at around 10 knots, and by trial and error we learned how the bucket could have a positive effect.

As a wave approached, I would bring the bucket right down, forcing the bow into the sea as the wave tried to pick us up. It was working – the slamming was being reduced.

Up until now we had been nearing a point where we knew something would give way soon. The boat would not be able to take this sort of punishment for ever. Something would go. The engine was labouring under the pounding the hull was taking from these waves. And each whine we heard made us hold our breath until it regained its momentum. But the bucket helped: we were regaining some control over the ferocity of the sea.

This strengthened my resolve to keep helming until dawn. I seemed to have caught the rhythm and the feel of the waves. The boat was still upright and I wasn't going to let her go now.

My decision to helm was not about wanting to be a hero. I just didn't want to die.

I had only one goal in my head, and that was to pull the boat through the night and eventually into port. It wasn't even about being the best helmsman. I wasn't – Andy and Nige were probably better. But right there and then I had this thing under some semblance of control and my instinct said hold on.

So I did.

By 3 a.m., Mick and I were still firing on adrenalin in our determination to keep the RIB level. Every sinew in our exhausted bodies was reacting to the sea beneath us.

Suddenly, though, the boat was struck by two waves simultaneously. Two converging walls of water collided over us. The *Arnold and Son Explorer* lurched violently to starboard and began to corkscrew. I clearly remember thinking she was going over. But she rose up again. The three bodies in the sardine tin were lifted at least 4 inches off the soaking wet thin foam covering, then landed in a heap as the boat crashed back into the water.

Mick was literally washed off his seat, and the force of the water threw him on top of me. We both clutched at anything solid around us. In the dark, and in blind panic, I grabbed hold of the wheel again and frantically tried to guess where the next freak wave was coming from. We were like blind men in a boxing ring, alone and afraid, taking punches from every direction.

Over and over again we were picked up like a feather on the swell and then dropped back to the water surface, with an impact equivalent to 7 tonnes of aluminium and fuel being dropped from the second storey of a house.

We had no idea how long our electrical equipment could withstand the combined effects of the relentless physical battering and the regular drenching by water pouring over the boat.

I was more frightened than I have ever been in my life, yet I have never wanted so desperately to live.

Our forward speed was almost zero, and we still had such a long way to go. The weather was getting worse, not better, and I wondered how much longer we could stay upright.

And what if we capsized?

I recalled how in diver training we had been told we would be able to survive for about fifteen minutes in the waters of the North Sea. We would have much less time up here in these icy seas just south of the Arctic Circle. We knew the drill: to try to clamber to the stern of the boat, which would then be upside down. Then keep together. But if you were separated in the capsize, the bottom line was that you would be lost to the waves. You would die.

I remember looking back at Charlie and seeing a look of terror on his face. He was ashen-white. His eyes looked a million miles away. They stared at me blankly. Empty. He didn't even bother to spit the water away from his mouth as the spray hit him in the face. He just lay there, beyond caring.

Nige was in the deckchair. He was holding his knife in one hand and his flares in the other. He looked deadly serious and truly scared. I looked back to the helm. I had seen all I needed to in those three brief seconds.

Time was moving so slowly, but everything was hurtling through my head at treble speed. I suddenly saw familiar faces in the sea and the waves. I reached out to touch Mick. I just needed to know he was there.

I was tiring. I had to be stronger.

The only light on the boat was a dull green glow from the

screen but it was enough to see what I had spotted. Glued to the edge of the console was a small, laminated photograph of Shara, holding our little Jesse; and she was smiling at me.

I had never felt in such danger of not seeing them again. I felt sick. I stared at Jesse, my little son. It broke my heart. 'How have I got into this situation?' I murmured. 'I promise you I will come home. I will see you again.'

I started muttering even louder to myself, almost talking out loud. I was speaking to Shara. My love.

'I will get this boat back safely. I will get back to you. Watch me, baby, this one last time.'

Shara has always believed in me. She thinks I am stronger than I am. She thinks I am nicer than I am. She defends me and always takes my side. If I am annoyed with someone, so is she. If I am exhausted, she soothes me. She makes me calm when I am nervous. And I have always loved her. She's my buddy. I would not break the promise I had made her at Heathrow.

Together, we had the world to live for. We had a son.

My mind raced back to that afternoon when little Jesse was born. I remember so vividly how people had warned me against watching my wife give birth: 'It's so animalistic,' they said.

It was a strange word. Yet every ounce of me wanted to be alongside her. It was our time, the biggest moment of our lives, and I knew we should be together.

It felt as though the world was standing still. I sat there

and held her as she writhed in pain. In her weakness, she somehow looked so strong, so feminine, so pretty. Not animalistic. I was witnessing so much more than the birth of a child; I was also watching the birth of a woman. Shara.

This was my family, all I had ever dreamed of, and the two of them both looked so frail as they lay there wiped out, exhausted. We had always wanted to call him Jesse. Shara said it was after King David's father in the Bible. King David had been quite a player. He even killed a giant called Goliath when he was only a kid. I liked the name though because it reminded me of Uncle Jesse in *The Dukes of Hazzard* – in dungarees, with a big white dirty beard.

But Jesse also means 'God's gift'. That felt so right to us.

As I watched them both sleep in the hospital, I was overwhelmed by a feeling of protectiveness. I would do anything for them; I would even die for them. I had never felt that before.

And right here, in the pitch black of the storm, utterly drained, sodden and frightened, I felt as though I was being asked, 'Could I now live for them?'

'**Come on, Bear,** we'll get through this,' Mick shouted in my ear, thumping me on the back. 'We've been through worse than this and come out alive. We'll do it again. We'll just get through this ... then we'll never go anywhere again!' And he slapped me once more.

Then Mick rummaged through the sodden food sack and pulled out another can of Red Bull. He swigged at it, then lifted my visor. I opened my mouth and tilted my head back so he could pour the liquid caffeine down my throat. It went everywhere.

'Come on, Bear, you're doing great, keep going! We can do this, buddy. Just keep going.'

Adrenalin was still surging through our bodies as on and on, through the night, we kept shouting at each other, punching each other, encouraging each other. And somehow we kept going.

Ever since Mick and I were eight years old, playing around in the Isle of Wight, there has been a bond between us. That bond was built through school, strengthened on the cold south-east ridge of Everest when he so nearly died; and now it was being reforged in the icy, choppy waters of the frozen North Atlantic.

While we were fighting our own battles at the console, there were three other men on that boat, huddled in the sardine tin, desperately trying to cope with their own worlds of terror inside their heads.

Charlie recalls:

For ten hours or so, I was absolutely convinced I was going to die. It was not just a question of being afraid; rather, an utter conviction that I was near the end.

It was not a question of 'if'; it was rather a matter of 'when', because I really believed the boat was going to flip.

Strangely, I had thought about this kind of near-death experience in advance. Before the expedition, I would get fit by running in the streets around my home in Manchester and, whenever I needed to motivate myself to push harder, I just imagined I had been thrown into the freezing water and I was swimming to get back to the boat. That image was very clear in my mind, and now it seemed to be about to happen, for real.

In some ways, the thought of drowning had always sounded quite relaxing. That's a bit morbid, I know, but the idea of being in the water, floating away, being numb to everything, thinking how nice it was not to have to worry about the bank manager – I must admit that I found that whole concept to be quite relaxing.

However, when it came to the crunch, the human instinct for preservation did kick in. I remember deciding I really did want to do quite a lot of things before I die. I didn't want to die here and now. I was not going to give up lightly. I was quite surprised by this. I thought of my immediate family: that kicked in, and very strongly. It was practical, not emotional. It was my decision: I didn't want to die. I wanted to get through this.

For me, time passed quite quickly. If you tell someone to sit in the corner, the first ten minutes go slowly, but then the hours pass quickly; and I wasn't really aware of Bear and Mick although I could see them hitting each other and shouting at each other. When things had started getting serious, they had gone all military; they were both practical and impressive, but I was still terrified.

Huddled beside Charlie, almost indistinguishable in a cold, wet heap, Nige shook with the cold and with his thoughts.

He recalls:

I understood Bear's decision to helm through the night. He felt that was what he had to do in the circumstances, and, from my point of view, well, it meant I didn't have to move – it was a bit of a result.

My main concern, though, was that the boat would flip, and I was trying to plan how I would get out of the boat from where I was lying. I imagined it would happen very quickly, and my strategy was to get myself around the back of the boat, pull the life raft out from where it was stowed and then help any of the guys who might be caught inside. We would set off our EPIRB distress signals, and call for help on the VHF radio.

This was my plan, but, lying there in the sardine tin, I knew it would be futile. If that boat flipped, there was no doubt at all that there would have been five dead bodies in the ocean. That is for certain. We were more than 200 miles from land, and there was no sign of any other shipping in our vicinity.

I didn't know exactly what it would take to make the boat go over, but it felt as if it was going to go over at every wave. It was going upright, and slamming down; then we would get hit from the side. I have never wanted to be somewhere else so much. I'm not religious, but I did find myself asking for someone to help us.

I prayed. We all prayed. We were praying for our lives.

And, somehow, we kept the boat upright.

Dawn seemed never to arrive. It was the blackest night I had ever seen. Mick and I would imagine the dawn ahead of us, to the east. We would then be convinced we could see it. But it was always an illusion; or worse, another wall of white water.

We knew that dawn would bring the light with it, and that would mean we would be able to read the seas once more.

Finally, though, the night sky began to brighten in the east. Together, shoulder to shoulder, Mick and I watched as dawn crept slowly over the distant horizon. The wind was just as strong, and the waves were just as menacing; we were still in danger, but we knew that our greatest enemy, the darkness, was disappearing before us.

My eyes settled on one of the laminated sayings stuck around the boat. It had been placed on the console just beside the photograph of Shara and Jesse and read, 'Each day ends so that a new beginning can be made.'

As the early morning of Friday, 8 August 2003 dawned over the Denmark Strait, it was indeed a new beginning.

I asked Mick to get all the guys up and huddle round. I wanted to encourage them. We could get through this now. There was hope. We had been through hell together, but I felt we were emerging out the other side.

So we cramped together, all of us freezing cold, the others squatting behind us on the edge of the sardine tin. I felt the cold chill of dawn on my face as I turned to them. It was 5.15 a.m. We were all exhausted and bedraggled, wearing full gear and helmets, squashed on this small boat in the midst of a still-heaving ocean.

'OK, guys,' I began, shouting again to make myself heard. 'First of all, I am sorry that I broke the rota. I found a way of handling the boat, using the bucket to control her, so I wanted to keep going rather than stop in the middle of the night and have to explain how we could each do this.

'I know it's been a tough and bloody cold night for

everyone, but we're going to get through this. It's daylight now. The sea has just lost its greatest ally – the darkness. There is no reason why we shouldn't make it out of this. We're going to reach Iceland.

'Only two things will stop us.

'The first is that we run out of fuel. But there is no need for this to happen. Andy has control of this, and we have enough to reach Iceland. But, Charlie, help him. Look out for him. Get him something to eat. Help him manage the fuel systems. Andy, we need all your skill and attention for these last few hundred miles.'

Andy nodded.

'The second is that we flip the boat. But I am telling you, we will not flip her if we concentrate and helm her correctly. We *will* flip if anyone loses concentration. Whoever is helming needs to be 120 per cent alert. There was margin for helming error before; that does not exist in this sea state.

'From now on, we go back to the rota. Everybody will helm for only half an hour at a time now, and we must help each other. We must all dig deeper than ever before. If we do this, we *will* reach Iceland before nightfall.'

Then I took a couple of minutes with everyone in turn, to show them how we could minimize the slamming by adjusting the position of the bucket over the jet. They all saw our defiant, plucky RIB respond, hugging the breaking waves as she punched through them.

Charlie later described my whole speech as 'almost Churchillian'. I'm not sure that's quite true, but I was just trying to keep everyone hanging on in there, just a little bit longer.

Mick and I were exhausted by now, and we collapsed into the sardine tin. Nige and Andy began to share the helming. Charlie had told me he didn't want to take the responsibility at this stage. I respected him for saying that. It was time for Andy and Nige to become the most important men on the boat, with our lives in their hands. And Charlie, as ever, kept their spirits up by feeding them chocolate and water.

Together, we had survived our longest night.

Back home in England, our friends and families were starting what would very soon become their longest day.

11. LOST AND FOUND

**Do not be terrified; do not be discouraged,
for the Lord your God will be with you,
wherever you go.**

Joshua 1:9

We had said we would call the base team at 8.30 a.m.

This was impossible.

As we had feared, the physical battering had taken its toll on our equipment, knocking out the compass, the radio and the SAT phone. The five of us had somehow survived the night of Force Eight gales, but, one by one, our carefully installed electronic systems had packed up and died.

By dawn, only the Simrad plotter and the Caterpillar engine were still in working order. And without the power to charge the SAT phone, we had no way of making these vital calls back to the UK. Our families, friends and our UK base would hear nothing, and there was little we could do.

The waves were still dangerous and wild, and the wind was still holding at gale strength; even in the daylight, when we could see the waves, we were fighting to survive.

Without precious electrical power, we had no way of telling if our tracking device was working.

It wasn't. We had dropped off the screen completely. Just like that.

It subsequently became clear we had lost power at 3.16 a.m.; that was the time when the tracker unit had stopped transmitting the signals, indicating our precise position and speed.

We knew that many people, up to 30,000 a day, and most importantly our friends and families, had been following our progress, live, through the website. They had grown accustomed to logging on and checking our latest position, as broadcast by the tracking unit every thirty minutes. At 3.16 that morning, the blips stopped and we effectively disappeared.

Back home, people were waking up and could see clearly that there was some kind of problem.

Shara recalls:

I had become obsessed with tracking Bear's position on the Internet. I was staying with my mother in the country, and she had become obsessed by it as well. So we got up at about quarter to eight on the Friday morning, and logged on as usual. But something was wrong. Their position had not been updated since 3 a.m. I thought that was a bit weird, but then there had been the odd little gap before, so I didn't panic.

I called Chloë, and she said not to worry. She told me Mick had called at two thirty in the morning, and had promised they would phone her again at eight thirty. She didn't say what Mick had told her about the storm. So I assumed all was OK. Chloë promised she would give me a call as soon as she heard from them.

I was busy getting Jesse ready because we were driving up to London for his eight-week check-up, but I noticed half past eight come and go with no call from Chloë. I didn't want to be a nuisance, but I was just beginning to get a bit concerned, so I called her at nine thirty. She told me they had still not called.

Chloë found herself in the midst of a nightmare. She was speaking to the families, assuring them everything was OK, explaining that we had been warned that the tracker unit might not function so far north; maybe that was all that was wrong. She was also trying to supply Captain Pennefather with the information he needed to work out what had happened to us. She was in at the deep end and was desperately worried.

Andy Billing was at his post on our barge, and he threw himself into sourcing relevant information, narrowing down the possibilities. He spoke to the team at MarineTrack, the manufacturers of our tracking system, and they posted a reassuring message on their website, explaining the system might be disrupted this far north. Chloë contacted Shaun White at Ocean Dynamics, seeking information about the electrical systems on the boat. He gave her the telephone number of the electrician at Mustang Marine who had actually fitted the systems, but he was away on holiday.

Meanwhile, we were continuing to make slow, steady progress in heavy seas, oblivious to the fact that back home, so many individuals were getting very nervous in an effort to track us down.

As soon as Captain Pennefather logged on to the Internet at 6 a.m. and saw our tracker had gone down he swung into action. This was his moment. He had always said that if we were in trouble he would drop everything and take over. He understood the sea and the procedures better than Chloë or Andy. And I always knew he would be there in the background – ready.

Willie recalls:

The analysis started at six in the morning, and it was crucial that we made the right calls. The Icelanders were only going to dispatch a rescue team if we asked them, and if we agreed to pay for it. Right from the start of this long and demanding day, the ball was in our court.

My first thought was that the crew had not put out an EPIRB emergency call, so the chances were they were OK. I was not overly concerned, even when Bear didn't call at eight thirty, as he had promised. Although I did remember mentioning to the crew before they left that I reckoned if the boat was turned over in a storm, it would be pretty bloody hard to swim and set that EPIRB off, but all the same, I tried not to go down that road yet.

We discovered the voltage on their tracker had been slowing over a period of hours and that if they had lost their electrics, this would explain not only why the tracker unit was dead, but also why they were unable to make any calls on the SAT phone. By mid-morning, the people at Iridium told us the crew had tried to make a call at ten thirty, but no connection had been made.

Of course, we were dealing with probabilities. Anything could have happened out there, and the base team, specifically Chloë and Andy, did a tremendous job holding things together this end.

I had indeed tried to call, albeit a bit later than scheduled, but conditions were not very conducive to phone calls in that storm. We had gone through the procedure of slowing the boat, and then I had crawled into the cubbyhole again and unwrapped the receiver with wet, shaking hands. I had tried and tried, but the connection never happened. I felt desperate. I tried again, to no avail.

I never found out why it failed. But I had no choice but to give up. All we could do was keep going and pray.

Friday, 8 August was unfolding as the hottest day of the year in London, with temperatures touching over 100°F. Out in the Denmark Strait, it was freezing. The high was sitting comfortably over the UK and it wasn't shifting. This was resulting in very deep depressions and low pressures up where we were, 1,000 miles north. We were shivering and wet. The sea was still a confused mess of white horses, hitting us from every angle, but Andy and Nige were doing an amazing job at the helm, keeping the boat in the right direction, withstanding the towers of freezing water that collapsed over the boat every now and then.

Everyone was emotionally and physically exhausted, but we were ploughing on, occasionally now boosting our speed to 14 or 15 knots, but then dropping again to 8 or 9.

We didn't speak much, but I felt that the night's terror had eased. We knew deep down that if we kept our heads, we would be able to reach Iceland in safety.

Unfortunately, back in the UK, there was still no evidence to help Shara and everyone else reach that same conclusion. She fought her way through the traffic coming up to London, but with Jesse hot, uncomfortable and frequently crying in the back of the car, she was starting to feel the strain of uncertainty. She couldn't even begin to contemplate the worst.

Shara recalls:

I arrived at the barge just before eleven, and found Andy Billing there. The telephone rang, and I just took the call because I was standing nearest the phone. It was a man called Howard, from MarineTrack. He asked for Chloë; I said it was Bear's wife speaking. He explained that the battery had probably failed. He couldn't tell me why, but it was pretty obvious, even to me. Batteries go wrong when they get wet. But I knew that their batteries were designed specially for the boat. So what had happened? I didn't even want to think about a capsize in those seas.

I just carried on, but was getting in more and more of a state. It was such a hot day, and I hadn't really eaten. I took Jesse to the doctor and the check-up didn't go particularly well – they told me there was something dodgy with his hip. It was the final straw. I burst into tears. I sat in my car like this, crying in the rush-hour traffic all the way back to my mum's.

There was still no news when I got to my mother's house. I sat outside in tears. I called Chloë and said something must have gone wrong because Bear had said he would call, and if Bear says he will call, then he always calls. My legs were shaking under me.

Then my mum started crying, and I asked her, 'Why are you crying?' Then I cried even more.

Willie called to ask if I had phoned Sally, Bear's mother. I said I hadn't because they were all having their holiday on the Isle of Wight and I didn't want to ruin it; at least not until we had firm news, either way. I was just petrified – petrified that something really bad had happened.

As that long day wore on, the base team worked hard to keep our families as calm and reassured as possible under the circumstances. They worked out what they would say, making sure they got their facts right and synchronized.

Chloë, Andy and Willie agreed on the following: 1) Say the EPIRB had not gone off, suggesting there had not been any disaster; 2) Say the electronics had probably failed; 3) Point out that, although the tracker had failed at 0300, we had tried to make a satellite phone call at 1030, so at least at that time we were upright. 4) Stress that these conditions were manageable for any rescue services that might be employed.

One thing worried Willie. He had quietly done some research of his own with the Naval Weather Centre. The conditions at the time the systems went down, they told him, were gale force. That was all he needed, and he thanked them. He didn't even want to imagine what we were dealing with out there. He had been a Royal Naval officer for thirty-four years. He knew what the sea could do.

Meanwhile, we were ploughing on. Progress was slow, but progress was progress. However, I was starting to worry about Nige. He was looking sluggish and exhausted.

Nige had exceeded all my expectations of him since the start of the expedition. He had never experienced anything remotely like this before, but had never once grumbled or made a fuss. He had quietly got on with it and had been incredibly strong. Nige, to me, is the typically understated, uncomplaining, brave British hero. The kind that would have been on Arctic patrols during the war, dressed in a duffel coat on the bridge of some small naval vessel, for months on end, seeking no recognition, just doing his job . . . a genuine, quiet, funny, tough Brit.

At the end of the leg from St Mary's to Greenland, Nige had been absolutely exhausted and, just like the rest of us, he really needed that rest, which the appearance of the weather window then proceeded to deny him.

As a result, when we started out from Greenland, his boots were still damp and his body ached. He didn't moan, because that is not his nature; he suffered the discomfort in silence.

'Nige, how you doing, buddy?' I said, prodding his shoulders.

He stirred and murmured he was fine.

I lay with him for a while, sometimes holding him, just being close. We were struggling in these relentlessly massive, heaving seas, and the wind was still freezing. But by going from minute to minute, hour after hour, through what amounted to the most terrifying period of any of our lives, we had survived together. We were not safe yet, but we were no more than 120 miles from Iceland.

Nige recalls:

Feeling cold was one thing but I was beginning to hallucinate as well. I was dozing in and out of sleep, and having really powerful, vivid dreams. At one point, my parents were beside me. At another time, in the height of the storm during the night, I had seen the most bizarre image: I could very clearly see an old man sitting on the side of the boat. He was in his seventies, wearing a yellow jersey and beige trousers, and he looked curiously like

Bob Hope! He seemed to have come down a rope ladder and, even though it was raining, he was completely dry.

'Do you want to come with me?' the old man asked.

'No. I don't think so,' I replied.

Then he smiled and disappeared. I wasn't sure whether it was an angel or whether it really was Bob Hope! It was odd, but it was OK. I wasn't concerned after this.

I just wanted to be warm and dry.

Looking back, I am certain that at critical times, when we needed it most, a presence, a guardian angel, was looking over us. I think we all felt it that night, and it was comforting. Maybe there is much more going on out there, around us, than we realize. I hope so.

Huddled close to Nige, I reached out for the Dictaphone. My hands were still shaking, and my skin had turned completely white, as if it had been submerged in a bath for three days – which I guess we all had.

Nothing was easy, even turning the Dictaphone on with shaky fingers. Time seemed to be passing so slowly. All I wanted was for this leg to be over, to reach Iceland, phone home and tell Shara all was OK. I had not spoken to her since Tuesday night, and this was almost Friday night. I knew she would be getting desperate, with no contact for so long.

Every word was an effort, as I spoke slowly and deliberately:

My God, this has been intense. We have been through so much together. Everyone is tired, and nothing works. The SAT phone and radio are dead. We have been through hell, and are coming out the other side. I think it was Churchill who said: 'When you go through hell . . . keep walking.'

That's what these guys have done. I'm so proud of them. They're just normal guys, but they have been put in these terrible conditions, and they have come through with real courage. They are not professional explorers or adventurers. They have normal jobs, and will go back to them and no one will have any idea of what they have been through. 'Good summer, Nige?' they'll probably ask him back at work! But these guys have been bloody brilliant. Quiet, brave, terrified, yet even cheerful . . . in short, just bloody brilliant.

I turned back to Nige. He had opened his eyes and was looking a bit better.

'Nige, you're not getting too cold, are you?' I shouted from behind my visor, above the roar of the engine. 'Can you move your fingers and toes all right?'

'Not really,' he replied. 'My toes have been numb since the Labrador.'

This wasn't good. The sardine tin was not the best place to hold a detailed medical conversation, but it transpired that Nige had experienced no feeling in his fingers or toes since the first storm, on our way over to Greenland. He had had no time to recover in Nanortalik, and his condition was deteriorating.

'Bear, what do you think is wrong?' he got around to asking me a few days later.

'It sounds like you've got frostnip,' I replied. 'It's not as bad as frostbite, but it's still pretty horrible.'

'Oh,' said Nige, 'and how long does it usually take to get better?'

'Well,' I replied, pausing because I knew this was going to be a bad one, 'usually for ever. It rarely gets much better.'

'Ah, thanks, buddy,' Nige replied, smiling. 'Great bloody bedside manner you've got.'

Typically, Nige now reflects and says he doesn't mind too much if he regains all the feeling in his toes or not. He is not in pain and, as he points out wryly, at least he will always have something to remember the Labrador Sea by.

I always remember someone once telling me that high mountains and big oceans often leave us with something to remember them by. Maybe this was the Labrador's legacy.

Back in the UK, Captain Pennefather knew that darkness was barely three hours away for us. He was drawing nearer and nearer to the moment when he would have to decide whether or not to dispatch the rescue services to hunt for our RIB.

There was still no news from us; the day seemed to be drawing on for ever, and all our families were now extremely concerned. Except the Grylls, because nobody wanted to ruin their holiday in the Isle of Wight! Until there was news, everyone would keep quiet.

In fact, the first that my mother heard about something being wrong was via a news placard outside the local news-agent. It was written in badly spelt English, and the headline simply read: 'Artic [sic] heroes in terror storm.' Whoever wrote it must have seen it on the newswire from one of the agencies keeping track of us, live.

My poor mum, who ever since Dad passed away always came back to the Isle of Wight for her summers, to relax, was back in the deep end. She couldn't believe that once again her son was in such trouble. Her sky had just turned black, and she rushed back to the house to find Lara, my sister, for some support.

Mick's parents also happened to be in the Isle of Wight at the same time, and news now began filtering through to everyone very fast. They were frantic, and all getting desperate for more news. The bright summer day was becoming less rosy by the minute.

However, the judgement call still rested firmly in the lap of Captain Pennefather, now on his mobile, on his boat in the hot Solent.

Willie recalls:

Chloë and Andy had been in contact with the Icelandic coastguard, requesting information on any search-and-rescue vessels available in the area, both sea and air. By mid-afternoon, the coastguard said they would send out a rescue team, but hinted where the financial costs would fall. It would be on us. Decision time, they suggested, was by 1900 hrs. This would give them time to reach the boat's last known position and return by nightfall.

I felt they were being too hasty though. The seven o'clock deadline was based on sending the team in a helicopter, but I felt it would be equally effective, and cheaper, to send a fixed-wing aircraft. On top of this, they would be able to cover a much greater search area in less time.

We were continually assessing the balance of probabilities throughout the day, and were greatly helped by the staff at the Fleet Weather Centre, who supplied up-to-date forecasts of the wind speed and direction, the wave heights and the currents, all of which enabled us to make a full analysis.

In the end, taking everything into account, we agreed to hold off until just before seven thirty in the evening. If there was still no news, we would send out a fixed-wing aircraft.

For this we would have to bear the financial costs.

When this news reached Mick's parents on their mobile, they were shopping in Tesco's. They were told the cost, and Mick's mother, Sally, replied plainly: 'Whatever it takes; we'll remortgage the house. This is our son's life.'

Chloë and Andy Billing remained together at the barge, supporting each other throughout the day.

Chloë recalls:

It was a really surreal time for us. We were sitting in the home of this crazy adventurer surrounded by his family photographs, all these images of smiling happy times, and all I could imagine was Bear and the crew in real trouble on those Arctic seas. We had to do everything possible to bring them home safely. But, in reality, we could do so little.

Shara recalls:

By half past six in the evening, I was in a terrible state. A friend rang and asked how everything was going, and I replied: 'It's not looking that great, actually.' I was panicking. I had these images of Bear's body floating around in the ocean, bobbing away, face down, and I began wondering how Jesse and I were going to cope without him. My imagination was racing out of control.

Then I spoke to my sister and almost convinced myself that Bear would never be coming back. I was in shock really.

I had to do something, so I phoned Willie and said he had to send out the rescue plane immediately. I said I knew that he and Chloë had Bear's best interests at heart, but they were not attached to him like I was. I was being a bit bossy, but we needed to know what had happened. I just felt that a delay could be fatal.

Out on the ocean it was early evening, and Andy and I were staring hard at the plotter. It clearly said we were just thirty-six nautical miles from Iceland. Together, we raised our eyes and stared straight ahead into a grey gloom of indistinguishable sea, spray and cloud, and we saw nothing.

'This is strange,' Andy said. 'We were able to see Greenland from sixty miles away. Where is this place?'

Andy rechecked the screen, then looked ahead once more.

'Is there any way the instruments could be wrong?' I asked.

'I don't think so,' he replied.

'This is so odd.'

Maybe the reading was wrong. Maybe something had gone wrong when we lost power. Maybe we had to recalibrate the GPS plotter after a power loss. My head was racing. I was exhausted and emotional, and I just wanted this struggle to have been worthwhile. I didn't want to have gone through all this and then, at the end, find we were in the wrong part of this vast ocean, because of an electronics error. I wasn't sure we could cope with another crisis.

Where was Iceland?

It was a grey, overcast evening, and it was drizzling persistently, but it wasn't foggy and the visibility wasn't too bad. It was just murky. We really should be able to see something as big as Iceland. We all stared at the plotter, and held our breath as the miles ticked away. It was strangely surreal.

We carried on through the rain, the *Arnold and Son Explorer* bounding forward now through the decreasing swell. We were all up, gazing ahead, straining our eyes, searching for the first sight of land.

Charlie asked, 'What does the plotter say now?'

'Twelve miles,' Andy replied.

We still saw nothing. We were all beginning to believe we had missed Iceland.

Nige was back in the sardine tin and he wasn't looking good. I glanced round at him. He just looked cold and wet and gaunt.

'We're pretty bloody close now, Nige,' I leaned over and told him. He smiled and pulled the sodden tarpaulin up to his waist, as if it was a duvet, not a soaking wet bit of thin material. He curled in tight, not really dozing, just existing. I moved across and pulled the tarpaulin higher – not that it made much difference.

But where was Iceland?

Slowly something appeared, dark and defined on the horizon. Nobody said anything. We weren't sure. A minute or so passed. This something looked vast and bleak. It was land. It was Iceland, and the lee of the Reykjavik Peninsula.

I suddenly felt an incredible surge of elation. We had all been through so much, and we had survived.

Together.

I grabbed Andy's shoulders and hugged him. Through these last few day, when all of us had really started to feel the effects of no sleep, he had emerged as a quiet, brave, true professional. I knew it had been worth keeping Andy's strength for the last quarter of this ordeal. We had needed him.

Andy recalls:

It had been a very long, hard crossing. To be honest, my real worry was the effect that the constant slamming of the waves would have on the material state of the boat. Any mechanical failure in these conditions would have been very serious, if not fatal.

We were very small against the vastness of the ocean all around us. It is very humbling; but the strong sense of teamwork gave me strength when I needed it. We were looking out for each other and focused on exactly the same goal – saving our arses!

It's hard to describe the feeling of relief when Iceland came into view but it meant that for the first time in days, I could stop listening to the tone of the engine and transmission with a critical ear. Constantly listening and desperately trying to detect any sign of problems had been both draining and at times very worrying.

It was my job to keep the engine going and, with a bit of luck, the bottom line was that Iceland was now just ahead.

Time was moving on back in the UK, and Captain Penne-father was on tenterhooks.

Willie recalls:

Soon after seven o'clock, I decided to call the coastguard in Iceland myself. I wanted to ask him if he was able to see a small yellow boat at all from their observation point. I thought he would be able to see fifteen miles out to sea.

He replied he couldn't see much. He said there was low cloud and steady drizzle, and visibility was poor. I had not had that information before, and that was enough for me.

I cracked. I decided that, if the pilots of a fixed-wing aircraft were going to have a chance of finding them in those conditions, they would need every minute of daylight they could get.

The boys had been tired, emotional, and frightened, and that had been when Chloë last spoke to them on the telephone sixteen hours before. I could only imagine what they were like now. I decided we had to send out the search plane. At the very least, the boys needed to know we were there, monitoring their position; on top of this, the families were desperate to know their husbands, sons and brothers were safe.

This longest day was reaching a dramatic conclusion.

19.26: At an airfield in Reykjavik, a fixed-wing aircraft is wheeled out of its hangar and prepares to fly out towards a precise position in the Denmark Strait, the position broadcast by our tracker unit at 0316 hrs that Friday morning, the very last positional broadcast before power failed. The pilots have been told to search for five British men, who are hopefully still aboard a small, open, yellow rigid inflatable boat.

19.28: Bear is sitting up in the bow of the boat; they are now only three miles from the west coast of Iceland. The SAT phone still has no power. Nige has been looking at his mobile phone, waiting to come within range of an Icelandic network, to get a signal. It eventually happens. He shouts to Bear and hands him the phone, still in its watertight pouch.

Bear scrolls down to the name 'Chloë Boyes' in the menu, and clicks the call button.

19.29: Chloë and Andy Billing are sitting at the kitchen table on the barge, relieved that at last a decision has been made. The rescue aircraft will be on its way anytime now. They wait and hope that this stomach-churning uncertainty will soon be resolved.

Suddenly, Chloë's mobile starts to ring. She looks down and sees the name 'Nigel Thompson' flashing on the screen, and all of a sudden she feels as though her heart has thudded against the inside of her ribcage.

'Hi, Chloë, it's Bear. I've got reception on Nige's mobile.'

'Where are you?'

'About fifteen minutes from the coast of Iceland.'

19.30: Andy phones the Icelandic coastguard and tells them to call off the fixed-wing aircraft. The message is relayed to the pilots, and they taxi back to the hangar, maybe relieved, probably irritated by the false alarm. They were on the tarmac, waiting for clearance to take off. Their flight was aborted with seconds to spare.

19.31: At her mother's house in the country, Shara is talking to her sister on the mobile. Desperate. The house phone rings, and her mother takes the call.

'They're fine, Shara,' she screams down the corridor. 'They're safe.'

Mother and daughter embrace, still in tears, but no longer tears of fear. Tears of relief.

It was almost 7.50 p.m. when we eventually pulled into the main harbour of Reykjavik. There wasn't even a ripple on the water now, just the pitter-patter of lightly falling rain. It was gloomy and the light was fading.

A lone fisherman emerged on the deck of a big icebreaker moored in the harbour. He waved nonchalantly. He hadn't any idea where we had just come from, or what we had been through. He carried on with his work, casually smoking. We idled on past. We couldn't quite believe we were finally here, alive.

I knew the Sir Ranulph Fiennes quote would still be wedged on the mirror in our bedroom back home. 'Them that stick it out, is them that win.' It was true. The only difference was that we had had no bloody choice but to stick it out. On this boat, there had been nowhere for us to hide.

I thought of home. I missed our cosy bedroom.

As we pulled alongside the wooden jetty in the marina part of the harbour, we began to set about the routine of tying up. Everyone was exhausted. Nobody was there to meet us because nobody had known where we were.

As Nige began to unpack some of the kit, he turned to me, smiling, and said, 'So guess which of our friends would have had the biggest fit if they had been out in the boat with us for five minutes last night?' Once again, he was chuckling to himself.

I thought for about one second only and then, in unison, we both looked at each other and said, 'Caroline and Shara.'

Shara's best friend, Caroline, loved sailing, but only with a gin and tonic in hand and a rather fit man in tight white trousers close by. The pair of them would have had the fireball of all fireballs in this boat all right. We laughed at the thought.

Moored alongside that quay in Reykjavik, our relief was written all over us. The spectacle of five men – dressed like yellow Michelin men, all of us pale, wrinkly and drained, clambering up on to the dock and crouching to kiss a jetty that stank of diesel and dead fish – was magical. We had done it.

But we had taken it to the wire.

Willie recalls:

I was mightily relieved they were safe, and also that the fixed-wing aircraft had been recalled before it took off to search for them. And I could now stop fingering Mick's American Express card, which was to be used as a guarantee for the flight!

Mick had proved himself almost unstoppable, but that bill, I suspect, would have wiped the smile off his stubbly face. He grabbed me warmly on the quay at Reykjavik. We had no idea of the drama that had unfolded at home, but we were on land at last. That was all that mattered.

The ice and the unpredictable Arctic seas were behind us. From here we would be heading down into northern European waters; we were no longer a million miles from home.

12. NO MORE HEROICS

Chance favours only those who know how to court her.

Hannibal

Sleep came easily in Iceland. We were all exhausted, in mind, body and spirit. Ever since we had arrived, the driving rain and wind had not relented, and we were just so relieved to be off the sea.

We went out that first night around midnight and found the finest steak-house in the city, where we drank cocktails without a thought of the expense. No one cared. We were safe, we were warm and we were together.

I had phoned Shara after we checked into the hotel and I was missing her like crazy now. As we ate and drank, I remember longing for her to be with us: celebrating, without a care in the world. I can't even remember what time we eventually got back to the hotel.

I would have given anything to have had Shara there that night, to put my arms around and sleep beside her – no offence to Nige, with whom I was sharing a room, but by now I had spent too many nights with him, curled up spooning in what had started to feel like a metal coffin on the ocean.

'The coastguards were pretty trigger-happy, don't you reckon?' Mick said, sitting around at breakfast the next morning. 'If we'd arrived ten minutes later, their plane would have been in the air and we would have had a bill for thousands.'

He was talking to himself as much as anyone. 'Then again, if you want anyone to be trigger-happy, it is them, I suppose.' That was true. He carried on eating his cereal.

The realities of what had been going on back home the previous long day, when we were out of contact for so long, were just starting to sink in. I felt terrible, and a bit guilty. But we had been lucky all round: lucky to have survived that storm and lucky that the rescue had been called off in time.

We had been let off the hook twice, once in the Labrador Sea and once off Iceland, and now we had to make certain we were safe. I was determined that we would not take any more risks on the two legs that remained, the first from Iceland to the Faroe Islands, and then from the Faroe Islands to the northern tip of Scotland.

Nobody wanted any more heroics.

We had slipped through the net twice, and we had been mightily humbled.

That day, as the white, flaky skin on my fingers was slowly beginning to regain a more familiar colour and texture, I slipped away to my hotel room, and spoke into my Dictaphone . . .

The others are still talking downstairs, and we have been in Iceland for nearly twenty-four hours now. We're slowly becoming human again. We're starting to hear other things apart from the diesel engine, and we all had these very vivid dreams last night. It's almost as if each of us is processing everything in our minds: the shock of what we experienced out there and the fact that we all felt a very real and genuine fear of dying.

I really want this to be over now. There is a kind of urge inside of me – to complete this properly, safely. I just want to get home. I don't want to put my crew through that kind of terror ever again. I don't want to look at Charlie, sitting in the deck-chair, his face literally white with fear, as if the spirit had been sucked out of him. I don't want to see the expression that spread across Nige's face when he saw the barometer plunge so dramatically. I don't want to have to find the reserves I somehow found when Mick and I helmed through the night.

It has been too intense and too exhausting.

We need a rest now and, when our minds are clear, we can plan these last two legs. One thing is certain: I'm not going out in bad weather or a head sea. I'm not gambling again. I want good weather and a following sea and, if we have to wait to get it, then so be it.

Everyone feels the same. Unless it is 100 per cent clear, wild horses would not get us back on that boat.

Once again, we were touched by the hospitality and generosity of the local people. Even people we met in the bars seemed to have been following our progress on the Icelandic TV news bulletins. Charlie was eager for conversation and, as he pointed out eleven times in one hour, 'My God, these Icelandic women are beautiful.' These words were invariably followed by: 'Excuse me? Hello . . . yes, I was the cameraman on board that boat, you know.' He was in heaven.

This paradise was slightly clouded though by the fact that our days in Iceland coincided with the Gay Pride Festival in town. The sight of us five, fresh off the boat, laughing, hugging and joking our way through the beers did rather limit the guys' chances with the ladies. As far as they were concerned we were quite plainly just five more Icelandic queens.

During our stay in Iceland, one man was more hospitable and generous than anyone before: a local boating enthusiast called Bogi Baldursson. He had not only read the news pieces but had even contacted our base in the UK and offered to help – with anything. Bogi took three days off work and virtually adopted us during our stay in Reykjavik.

'Bogi, we need help with this alternator.'

'No worries. A mate of my brother owns a big garage. I'll take you there.'

And he did.

Bogi also told us that we all looked terrible, white and exhausted. Thanks, Bogi, I thought. So he insisted that we should take a trip out to a natural springs spa, where Icelanders strip down to their undies and relax in the pure waters. Charlie remembered the calibre of the girls he had seen the night before and didn't need much encouragement to come along. But things looked less promising in that department when we were joined by a friend of Bogi's called Omar, who was physically vast and evidently well built in all areas. And it was with him that we would be sharing the spring. Ah.

On the drive back to Reykjavik, we were all talking.

'Bogi, some of our kit is still wet. The hotel staff are going nuts with it all everywhere. Do you know somewhere where we can get it dry?' I asked.

'Sure,' he replied. 'Omar can do it. He has a very big facility.'

I prodded Nige in the ribs, and neither of us could breathe for the next half hour.

Back at the hotel, we got serious again and started to address the real issue of getting the weather forecast right for the next leg: another 500 nautical miles through to the Faroe Islands. Our task was made easier by the fact that we would now be passing through comprehensively charted waters, where the availability of data meant the forecast was more accurate than the 'guestimates' we had been relying on in the Denmark Strait.

The guys at the Fleet Weather Centre were correct when they said Force Seven winds were running in this area at the moment. We could sit and watch the rain and wind beating at the windows. They also said it was because the high-pressure system was still settled over Britain, pushing more of these lows up to the north. They suggested conditions should improve later in the week and that, all going well, we would be able to get on our way by then.

Mick and I visited the Icelandic weather centre just outside of the city, and came back with the same picture of bad conditions at the moment, improving on Wednesday or Thursday.

Our third source of information to confirm this forecast was Mike Town; almost down to the last detail, he produced the same predictions as the two fully equipped, professional weather centres. If only the data from the previous two legs had been as consistent as now, but it had been almost impossible to predict the conditions on remote, distant oceans with 100 per cent accuracy. We had always known this was one of the major risks involved in the expedition, but Mike had done a professional and dedicated job for us. He had always given his assessment of the weather patterns diligently and cautiously. We had been very lucky to have him there for us, day and night.

'Right, guys,' I told the crew, relieved that for once I was not having to tell them we would be leaving at 5 a.m. the following day, 'it looks as if we have until Wednesday to get the boat right.' Each of them looked as though I had just placed a golden nugget in their hands.

The *Arnold and Son Explorer* was a mess: the electrics were down, there was water and diesel all over the place, and she looked as if squatters had been camping in her for a month.

Charlie and Nige set about the minor repairs, and Andy spent almost an entire day trying to resolve the electrical problem. His assessment was that when we had crashed down off a huge wave, the batteries had been thrown upwards and shorted on the aluminium. In due course, the boat-builders would hardly believe this – they had never known the actual stern of the boat to be lifted and thrown so violently by a wave as to catapult the batteries loose from their housing, but then not many of them had seen what happens to an RIB in a storm in the Denmark Strait. The fact that the batteries had been so dramatically dislodged offered a fair indication of just what the seas had thrown at us out there.

The result of this 'short' was that we had lost our entire 12V system, bringing down all communications. It could so easily have affected the engine management system as well, but in this respect, yet again, we had been lucky; it was as simple as that.

The more we examined the boat, the more we realized just how fortunate we had been. It was the strange sixth element of luck that no one can ever quite put a finger on – but we all knew it had played a huge part in what had happened so far.

With the help of Bogi and his mates, who were kind enough to open their garage out of hours and make sure all our batteries were fully charged, we got the electrical system up and running again. By dusk, the guys were still sorting out the kit and finishing some final minor repairs around the lockers and console but the RIB was slowly starting to look herself again.

While we were down on the quay, we met a round-the-world sailor, a Frenchman called Frédéric, who had just pulled into port from Scandinavia. He was preparing to cross to Greenland and was awaiting a break in the weather.

'What's it like out there?' he asked nervously.

'Oh, it can be a little bumpy at times,' Mick replied nonchalantly. Charlie shook his head, smiling.

We also met some of the crew of a large ice-going maritime research ship, the *Oreanos*, which had just made the same crossing from Greenland as we had, but about twenty-four hours later. They also said conditions had been horrendous, and told how the waves had been coming over their bridge. I looked up at their bridge: it was 35 feet up from the water.

I glanced across at Mick, and he glanced back at me. We had been let through by the skin of our teeth this time, but the sea doesn't always let you win.

We were looking forward now, though: we were going home. The unsettled weather had moved on, and after double-checking the forecast we agreed we would leave early on Wednesday morning.

Our last evening in Reykjavik was spent in the company of Ulruga Olassi, a mountaineer who had become the first Icelander to reach the summit of Everest three years before. He had read about our expedition and asked if he could come and have a look around the boat. In his late thirties, he was smart and kind-faced, and he obviously understood what we had been through. Both Everest and the big oceans make similar demands: they require heart, humility and a bit of luck to survive.

'Tell me,' he asked, 'why did you decide to make the crossing from Canada to Scotland? Isn't this against the current? It would have been easier the other way round.'

I explained that to be heading home, with each wave and each mouthful of seawater, was what really counted. I had always wanted us to be homeward bound.

He smiled, and understood.

To err on the side of caution, we had decided to include a refuelling stopover at the Vestmann Islands en route to the Faroes. These isolated patches of land out in the sea, some 80 miles from Reykjavik, would give us another opportunity to check the latest weather forecast, make sure we were clear to go, and ensure we completed this final stretch without any drama.

I didn't want any mistakes at this late stage. The highest mountains in the world are strewn with bodies of climbers who reach the summit but die on the descent, and so many war memorials list the names of soldiers who survived the main war only to die in the last few skirmishes.

We had to see this through. Properly.

Just before we left Reykjavik that final morning, I was tracked down on my mobile by Alex Rayner, our PR man, and minutes later, outside the hotel lobby, I was on the phone doing a live radio piece back to the BBC. In the interview, I was saying we hoped the weather would at last be kind to us.

'Yes ... we can hear the Arctic winds howling behind you,' the presenter said dramatically. He seemed a little surprised when I explained that the noise he heard was actually Reykjavik rush-hour traffic on the main road behind me. It wasn't quite the blast of icy winds he had hoped for!

Our last act in Iceland was to take Bogi and his young son, also, by good coincidence, named Bear, out on the boat for a quick spin around the harbour. This was to say thank you, and they both loved it. We would soon meet Bogi again, when he made a surprise visit to London to attend our homecoming party at St Katharine Docks. All the team's faces lit up when they saw him again. He had become a friend, and Nige couldn't resist asking how 'Omar's big facility' was doing. Bogi laughed.

Throughout the expedition, every day of departure had brought its own sense of tension, and the time for leaving Iceland was no different. The guys were quieter, and there were fewer jokes as we all focused our minds on getting everything ready. Now and then, someone would look up at the sky, just a little nervously, as if checking the weather one last time.

Part foreboding at what lay ahead, part excitement, part relief that we would soon be moving ever nearer home – these times were always special. There was a special atmosphere and, to be honest, they were almost the moments I loved the most. Just the team, all together, at work.

It was a few minutes after seven o'clock on a calm morning when we slipped our mooring in the Icelandic capital's harbour.

Light on fuel, because the Vestmann Islands were so nearby, we began to power through the gentle seas at 21 knots, which was a welcome change from the 12 knots we usually managed when we were heavy with diesel at the start of a new leg.

I reached for the Dictaphone, and spoke . . .

Everything is rock 'n' roll now. The boat is working well, and everything seems more waterproof in the lockers. Little things, like the problem of the drinking water that used to fizz out of the jerry cans inside the cubbyhole with all the slamming, have been solved. We are learning and getting better all the time.

I'm just praying this weather holds. I have such a strong memory of leaving Prince Christiansen Sound, and how beautiful and calm the sea was for twelve hours, and how it all turned so dramatically different after that. And it happened so fast. I'm a bit tentative about the 'good forecast' now and I sense the same hesitation in everyone else.

We're passing huge cliffs around southern Iceland, and we have a steady following sea. This is so good. I hope it stays like this. We're getting there. Come on!

Arriving in the Vestmann Islands, we found a stunning natural harbour surrounded by deep, lush, green grass that looked as if it had been glued to the dramatic, sheer cliffs. There was the usual stench of fish and there was an array of large fishing boats along the jetty. These boats were all tough and hardy, and proud, and they looked as though they were used to working in these ruthless and demanding northerly seas.

We refuelled as planned, while Mick put a call through to the Fleet Weather Centre. He reported back to say they had given us the all clear and were predicting westerly winds; that meant that the wind would be blowing from almost directly behind us right the way through to the Faroes. It was ideal. We would push straight on.

As we skirted round the last few remaining islands, the ice-capped plateau of southern Iceland appeared on the port side: huge, majestic and cold. We were soon surging through the gentle swell, trying to relax and settle into the familiar rota once more. As Iceland slipped away behind us, we just lapped up the natural beauty all around.

A school of dolphins appeared in our wake, cheerfully playing in the waves, and all kinds of birds seemed to fly overhead, as if to satisfy their curiosity about what such a small yellow boat was doing out here in these seas. This was what we had waited 2,500 miles for, and each of us savoured every precious moment.

But we still felt cautious. We had been here before, and if we had learned anything from this ocean, it was that the sea must always be respected, never taken for granted, always feared.

The sea knows no rules. It is a law unto itself, and it moves at will. It's this incredible force that is always heaving beneath you. Sometimes it can be magnificent; sometimes it can be brutal. But either way, it doesn't care. It just is. And when you begin to think you understand it, and have it taped, that's the time when it rises up in defiance. Even when it is calm, as it was when we were surging on towards the Faroe Islands, you can still sense the huge, silent force beneath you, and you fear what that force can do.

As I sat there and stared across the vast grey ocean, I sensed a strange kind of paradox. As individuals, we spend a short time on this planet. We exist, and try to follow our dreams and live with meaning, but the sea is different. It is so much greater than us, timeless, unending, relentless, and it just churns on, always evolving. In many ways, this makes it the supreme arena. And yet, even as we experienced this huge ocean, with its capacity for rage and ruthlessness, even as we felt so vulnerable to its whims, I somehow felt a part of it as well.

Why is it that storms are so often followed by periods of intense calm and quiet? Is this just coincidence, or is this the living ocean speaking to us, feeding us a small part of its vibrant life force? Surely it is touching our souls and desires, ever drawing us in, testing us.

Our frail dreams and survival instincts are also part of this natural world. We are human, after all, born from nature. We may not always feel welcome, but we are a part of the ocean as well. We have a small place here. Maybe that's what God intended: that in these quiet moments we should understand we are not utterly insignificant, but are in fact special. We belong, and we each have a home in this vast corner called 'nature'.

Perched on the prow of the boat, alone with these thoughts, heading south-east, I had time to reflect and to feel. I realized then that maybe I have two homes: one back in England, with Shara and Jesse, where we are together, holding one another, warm and safe; and the other out here in this wilderness, feeling tiny among the elements, but living, and free. Maybe it is these two parts, these two homes, that make up the person I am.

All of a sudden I was brought back to the here and now by the sound of laughter from the console area. I could see Andy trying to teach Charlie magnetic variations in northern hemispherical navigation. Charlie was looking confused.

Andy had always been very correct in using maritime terms: 'for'ard' and 'aft', 'windward' and 'leeward', 'sheet' and 'knot'. But throughout the expedition, Charlie never got this.

'What's wrong with "forward", "back", "left" and "right" and "rope" and "mph"?' he would insist, and now he finally cracked.

'Let me teach you about boats, the Manchester way,' Charlie continued with a wry smile, and he started stomping around the boat, using Andy's fuel-marker pencil to scrawl 'front', 'back', 'left' and 'right' all over the appropriate tubes.

Andy was cringing with despair. It was very funny.

Conditions remained calm as night fell and, for the first time any of us could remember, we were able to sit back and enjoy the most stunning of sunsets, as inch by inch the bright orange glow was consumed by the distant crimson and cobalt blue horizon. We sat and watched, lost in our thoughts and also in our memories.

Even on the night watches we sat transfixed, mesmerized by the simple beauty of the night under clear northern skies.

We had always expected the nights to be much lighter than usual during the expedition, but we seemed to have been followed by heavy clouds and most nights had been pitch dark. Now it was clear and we gazed up at the shooting stars and the full moon and marvelled at the phosphorus under the RIB's bow. Charlie and I were on watch together from 1 a.m. to 2 a.m. and for the first time, this 'graveyard' shift was an hour of sheer pleasure.

As dawn broke, we emerged into a few gentle squalls of rain, which softly pebbled the surface of the flat sea. Mick and I lay in the sardine tin in the rain, chatting about army days and holidays, and what we were going to do when we got home. It was the best of times. Even the soft rain was a joy.

We were less than a mile from the Faroes when they finally materialized through the cloud. Rough landscapes of hills and craggy rocks were interspersed with lush green pastures all around and we soon passed a huge, natural cave, worn in the cliff face by the relentless battering of the sea. It was remarkable, large enough to enclose a decent-sized house. We moved inside and sat quietly, all alone, silenced by nature's creation.

By the time we pulled into the small port of Thorshavn, it was raining heavily. The harbour was surrounded by rows of small houses, most of which were grass-roofed. Some of them were perched precariously on the cliffs.

A lady from the local sailing club came bounding down to greet us.

'Welcome to the Faroes,' she declared. 'Chloë has just called from London.'

Right to the end, our base team were on the ball.

'We have arranged for you to use the sailing club as a base to rest. Please treat it as your home. I hope that it is going to be all right for you.'

It was perfect. We could hang out our kit, drink cups of tea, and doze on the floor.

We ate well in the local bar, made the necessary phone calls to the base team and the weather centre and, before long, the five of us were settling down for a few hours' sleep in the sailing club's small upstairs room.

Within moments of the light going out, Charlie was snoring.

'I'm not sure which is worse,' Nige muttered in the darkness, lying awake on the floor, 'Charlie's nostrils or the roar of a 450-horsepower Caterpillar engine.'

He had a point.

13. SAFE IN SCOTLAND

We are the Pilgrims, Master; we shall go
Always a little bit further; it may be
Beyond that last blue mountain barred with snow,
Across that angry or that glimmering sea.

Special Air Service regimental verse

It was strange. I had spent most of the past few weeks doing everything possible within my grasp to reach the final destination of this expedition safely, and yet, now that we were only 275 miles from the north coast of Scotland, I found myself feeling almost sad that the end was so near.

We woke just before 3 a.m. and I became aware that we were probably pulling on all our kit and dry-suits for the last time. I looked around. The crew were quiet.

'OK, guys, I need your concentration for twelve more hours,' I told everyone as we stood in the cold night air, preparing to slip our mooring on the quayside for the last time. 'Twelve more hours, that's all. Let's just keep this boat pointing due south, steer a good course and make sure we don't make any stupid mistakes. If we just stay focused and do what we do so well together, then we will reach Scotland.'

We all knew what needed to be done.

'One last effort,' said Mick quietly.

There was a relief in us all, waiting just on the other side of the door. We were so close to achieving our target. But there was also a sense of loss that the spirit that had carried us through so many dangerous situations could not last for ever.

Of course, the five of us would stay in touch and see one

another whenever we could, and we would regularly look back and laugh, and feel proud of what we had done; yet the reality was that as soon as we touched British soil, the precious magic we all felt so intensely would begin to disappear.

That is just how it is.

'I'd love to helm this first bit, if that's all right?' Charlie asked. The night was glorious, and he took the wheel.

There was scarcely a breath of wind on the water, and the moon was reflected on the still harbour water around us. We untied the ropes and quietly left the Faroes.

We had decided to leave at 3 a.m. because the early departure meant we would reach Scotland in daylight, and therefore would actually be able to see the end of our expedition. Which would be nice!

In fact, we had originally planned to leave even earlier but Force Six and Seven winds had been blowing through the area to our south and our meteorologist, Mike Town, suggested we should wait until they had passed. We hoped they now had. Still determined to minimize any risks, we waited until the hour he suggested.

The few flickering lights of Thorshavn, the small town in the Faroes, were soon receding into the distance. We were yet again leaving behind people who had been incredibly kind and generous. What was it about these maritime communities that always made their reception of us so warm? It had become such a feature of this expedition: arriving in isolated communities as total strangers, and leaving as friends.

While we had been refuelling the previous evening, people had approached the boat freely, chatting, many of them
just wanting to touch the tubes and wish us well; and in
Thorshavn, as in so many other remote places we had been,
they had wished us 'calm seas and God's speed'.

But above everything, they all seemed to have time ...
time for us, time for themselves, time just to be.

That is what I hunger for: space, the time just to sit and
be. The freedom from the rush, the little moments, the ones
that we so often overlook and miss, even forget exist.

In supposedly more developed parts of the world, we have
so little patience. We want it all, and we want it now. We rush
from one thing to the next. We have no time for what really
matters, and our lives become a blur. How often do I struggle
to remember what I did yesterday, let alone last week? That's
terrible, really.

'So are you busy at the moment?' We hear it the whole
time, as if to be busy is something we should strive for. A
friendly everyday question, but it speaks volumes. I think we
are all so busy that we lose touch with who we really are.

'The heart of a man is like deep water,' I once read.
No wonder so many of us struggle with our identity. We
are too busy to find it, too busy to listen to those deep
waters.

Those men and women in Labrador who told us to stay
in port had tried to warn us and protect us from the northerly
winds we eventually ran into. But we had rushed ahead.

Perhaps I should have listened more.

On two occasions on the expedition, in St Mary's and then again in Nanortalik, we had rushed, and so nearly fallen.

We were powering ahead by the time dawn burst over the eastern horizon, reaching 22 knots in a following sea. It was just before 5 a.m. We were homeward bound and gradually starting to believe we would make it. I took the Dictaphone and carefully made my way to the foredeck ...

It's all looking fine. The forecasters predicted a following sea and good conditions, and that's what we have got. High winds have passed through this area now and all that remains are the cresting, driving waves behind us – the remnants of that bad weather. And the boat feels alive. She has been amazing. She feels somehow stronger now, as if forged by the wild seas to our north, so far behind us. I don't want to leave her. She did everything we ever asked of her, and I can't stop remembering that night at the start of the Boat Show back in January, where on my own I stroked her hull and prayed we would come through this together.

And she has never faltered.

I'm sitting at the bow of the boat, on my own, and the sun is shining more strongly than at any other stage of the expedition. The sea is rolling with us, and the boat is eating it up.

The guys have been brilliant as well. I think it's very rare to ask four mates to risk their lives alongside you for no reward except the bonds you create together in the hard times. To see those same men come up with the sort of courage and quiet fortitude I saw in them during those two terrifying storms is special. They have truly impressed me. They have risked everything over the past few weeks, and they have all over-delivered, and proved themselves stronger than I reckon they ever knew. That's a good thing to discover.

I received a message last night saying that I have been asked to appear on David Frost's Sunday-morning programme this week, but, as I sit here now, that kind of thing seems a million miles away. To be honest, I would prefer to be here with these guys, away from the bright lights of that weird world.

Deep down, all of us are dying to see Scotland. It's all we ever talk about.

My hour at the helm followed soon afterwards, and for most of the time my eyes seemed to dart from the seas ahead to the dial that indicated the number of nautical miles remaining on the leg, and I was lucky enough to be watching the dial when it ticked down from 100 to 99 miles. Charlie took the helm after me, and he seemed to be making good progress when Nige leaned forward and stared intently at the small screen on the console. The small arrow indicated the direction in which we were moving, and it was pointing 180 degrees the wrong way.

'Charlie, where are you going?' Nige asked.

No reply.

'Scotland is that way,' Nige said, pointing at the stern behind him, laughing out loud.

Charlie quickly realized his error and swung the helm around. He had been away in his own world for a few minutes and had lost concentration.

'Did you leave something behind?' Nige teased.

'Yeah, those Icelandic girls,' Charlie replied, chuckling. 'I can't get them out of my head.'

We were so close to home that even travelling in the wrong direction only made us laugh. 'How far to go?' I asked.

'Sixty-one miles,' Nige replied. 'Sorry, sixty-two now.' Charlie hit him.

An hour later, Mick was helming. Andy was asleep and Scotland was getting ever closer, but still remained out of sight. We should see it soon, I thought to myself.

Everyone else was quiet.

Then suddenly, as if from nowhere, I heard that terrible, fateful sound. I knew what was happening. The engine was dying, the revs were plummeting, the throttle was no longer responding to Mick's acceleration.

Within seconds, we were silent.

No, God, not this close, please no, I said to myself. Please.

Then I thought, no, it's all right. We'll be OK. It will be the fuel again. We can sort this. All we need to do is switch to another tank and get the engine going again. It should be easy. Shouldn't it?

Andy leaped into the engine bay and set to work.

Five minutes passed.

I glanced at Mick. He was beginning to look anxious. The process shouldn't take this long.

Eight minutes. Andy had switched the tanks over and had tried to reprime, but the engine wasn't responding.

We were still bobbing helplessly.

Ten minutes.

My mind was racing: How could we survive the Labrador Sea and cross the Denmark Strait in a storm, and then fail in this gentle following sea, just short of home? It must work. Come on.

Andy was working frantically. I said nothing.

Another turn of the key, still no splutter of life.

Twelve minutes.

Then, once more, a final turn of the key, a spark, a splutter, another splutter ... a roar, a fantastic surge of power. We had movement again.

'Just keeping you all on your toes.' Andy smiled.

We all were grinning, so relieved.

The miles started to fly by. Adrenalin was pulsing through us as we all gathered in the bows, with Nige helming, our eyes glued on the horizon. We couldn't quite comprehend that we were about to see the mountains of north Scotland. This moment had been so long in coming.

It was 2.20 p.m. when we finally spotted the distant purple outline of the mountains, dead ahead. We were still 33 miles from land, but the end was literally within sight.

This was the moment to phone Shara.

She had initially planned to travel north and meet us in Scotland, but moving Jesse when he was still so young and just getting settled seemed crazy. I had told her to stay at her mum's. It meant we would only have to wait a day longer to see each other again. In any case, I knew we would be so busy in Scotland, doing the press stuff and sorting out the boat. I was happy to wait another twenty-four hours and see them both in earnest at Gatwick airport. I had waited so long and travelled so far. I wanted our reunion to be perfect.

She answered on the second ring.

'We can see Scotland, my love,' I told her, struggling to hold my emotions, 'dead ahead, getting clearer as we speak. I can see Ben Loyal. You know, the mountain I dragged you up when we first met, and everyone else got vertigo. Remember? It's on our nose, straight ahead. I cannot wait to see you, my angel. I told you we would be OK, didn't I?'

I could hear the relief in her voice when she said gently, 'My God, this has been a bad one.'

I looked up at Ben Loyal ahead. It seemed to be watching us, willing us on. There was magic in the air.

The plan had always been to arrive in Scotland in this small estuary, near to the lodge belonging to an old friend of Shara's and mine.

Sam Sykes and his family lived in a small, remote part of Sutherland, on the north coast, at a place called Kinloch. Shara and I had met there, many years ago, at New Year. It was one of the best days I can remember. I had been staying up there with Sam, training and climbing. It was two months before the Everest expedition in 1998, and I had everything apart from girls on my mind.

I was climbing every day, pushing myself, preparing myself mentally and physically for the months ahead in the Himalayas. I was very solitary and focused, and probably a bit of a nightmare. Then this girl called Shara walked in, dressed in a tatty red coat, and life has never been the same.

Together, we made up silly dances, kissed in the woods and fell asleep on the sofa in our boots, with my big duffel coat over us. Kinloch would always be special to us both.

I had planned with Sam to have just a small band of family, friends and sponsors meet us 'unofficially' a few miles off Kinloch in his boat. We would then come in and spend a night at his lodge before heading back out the following morning and cruising along the coast to John O'Groats for the official homecoming.

To me, however, there was only ever going to be one real homecoming and that was our arrival here in Kinloch, with the five of us in the bows, staring ahead, gaze fixed, straining to see the outlying shadow of Rabbit Island at the mouth of the Kinloch estuary.

However, the plan wasn't quite going so smoothly at Sam's end. The two guys from Arnold and Son, Eric and Jean-Marie, were delayed in transit from Zurich to Inverness. Despite a mad dash in a small hired car that apparently resembled a scene from the film *Trains, Planes and Automobiles*, with these two smart Swiss businessmen racing like rally drivers along the narrow Scottish lanes, they couldn't reach this remote corner of Scotland in time to get aboard Sam's boat and meet us at sea.

So it was Chloë, Charlie's father, James Laing, Alex Rayner, Jamie Curtis, a cameraman, and Lorraine, Andy's girlfriend, who clambered aboard Sam's boat and ventured out, earnestly searching for us through the haze of rolling Scottish waves.

Linking up wasn't straightforward. For some time they couldn't see us, and we couldn't see them. Radio contact was intermittent and poor.

Eventually, Chloë spotted some spray on the horizon, and as we drew nearer, they saw what they hoped would be our small yellow boat on the horizon. Then radio contact became clearer and we heard Sam's voice over the intercom.

'I think we can see you,' he shouted excitedly.

The boat was dipping between the troughs of the waves, rolling in towards them. They waved frantically. We still couldn't see them. And then we could. A small blue dot to starboard. We came back on the radio and they heard our voice for the first time:

'This is the *Arnold and Son Explorer* to Sam – we have you in sight, we're coming home.'

We circled their boat, waving madly. Sam was going berserk, Chloë was shouting and Lorraine was crying. We had done it. We were almost there. Sam escorted us in towards a beautiful, sandy cove, and we drove the RIB up on to the beach. We killed the engine one last time, leaped ashore and hugged everyone, jumping up and down in the surf.

In the time it had taken for them to escort us in, Eric and Jean-Marie had finally arrived. Just in time. As they pulled up with a skid on the track above the beach, they saw the boat that their vision had made possible pull into the cove.

When I saw Eric, I ran across the beach to where he was standing. I just wanted to thank him for everything he had done to make this dream happen. However, as I went to hug him, and he squeezed me, my dry-suit released a stench of stale, unwashed body odour from my neck seal. It was horrendous, he told me later, laughing.

Through almost 3,000 miles on the ocean, it had been impossible to maintain any kind of personal hygiene in the RIB, even though, to his credit, Andy was meticulous in brushing his teeth every morning, wherever we were. For the most part, we just lived and slept and did everything in what we wore.

I hugged Eric again for good measure.

We then knotted several lengths of rope together so we could secure the RIB safely to the harbour wall, and began swigging from bottles of Mumm champagne. Eric toasted us, Alex toasted us, Andy kissed Lorraine (poor girl!), and the moment was perfect.

So, on this quiet Scottish beach, with just a handful of the most important people around us, we celebrated the safe return of our expedition. We had faced the frozen ocean, and we had survived. We were home and alive.

After a while, we drove up to Sam's house and threw our kit down in a heap. Then I wandered down to the small brook below his house, where Shara and I had so often swum together. The water was bubbling over the rocks into the pool. I stripped off, stood on the overhanging rock above the pool, and dived in. As I came up for air, I felt the emotion, the strain and the fear of the last two years wash off me. Literally. I couldn't help smiling. I had been so worried I would not deliver on my promise to Shara and return safely. But we had. I shook the water from my hair, took a deep breath, and went under once more.

While we had still been in the Faroes, during a telephone conversation Chloë had asked me if there was anything special we would like for dinner on our first night in Kinloch. There could only ever be one thing: roast beef with all the trimmings. And it was duly delivered.

We ate like kings – in fact, to be more specific, we probably ate like King Henry VIII, gnawing the finest beef off huge bones, laughing at the same old jokes and drinking far too much red wine. It was the best of meals – cosy, intimate and wild.

As we sat round that table in Scotland, I felt overwhelmed by pride at what we had achieved and enormous gratitude to be surrounded by such truly good people.

Everyone had their own private feelings on the expedition, drawing their own conclusions from what we had all experienced.

Charlie reflects:

Almost the first thing I said to my father when I saw him on the beach in Scotland was that I could hardly believe how five men could have travelled 3,000 miles in this tiny living space, and endured so much pressure and strain, and yet there had not been a single cross word between any of us.

The expedition was amazing for the bond that developed between us, but I think I most enjoyed the sense of being so alone with the elements. We were travelling in an open, rigid inflatable boat, and, in explaining what we went through, the most significant of those adjectives is certainly 'open'.

I only now appreciate what this really meant. There was absolutely no protection from the wind, the waves and the noise on that boat. Everything was in your face, all the time, soaking you, deafening you, numbing you, burning you.

Of course, it wasn't always fun. There were times when it was 100 per cent horrible. However, all in all, it has been the most mind-blowing experience. To be made to feel so vulnerable, but to survive – it's not a bad thing to go through.

People still ask me what it was like on the ocean, and the best I can do is say that it was like parking an open-topped people-carrier in a car wash, and living in it for two weeks with four other men, during an earthquake, in sub-zero temperatures.

Sometime later, my dad asked me if I thought I had changed as a person because of the expedition, and I gave him an honest answer: 'Not really.' I have just got on with my life. Maybe I have learned to appreciate things a bit more than before, but it's marginal. I just feel very lucky to have had this extraordinary opportunity.

Andy reflects:

In some ways, it all ended too quickly. I felt a bit like a chef who had spent so long preparing a meal, which was then eaten in twenty minutes. For me, sixteen days passed like twenty minutes.

It was a great experience. There were good times and hard times, but never bad times, although I did have a sense of foreboding when we set out for Iceland with bad weather ahead.

Looking back, I am certain the sea could have thrown even worse at us. I think we all realize we got away with it this time and, with one twist of the dice, it could have been so different. It might very easily not have been such a happy ending to such an exciting expedition.

None the less, we got home safely and, in the days ahead on HMS *Newcastle*, I have no doubt that I will miss the feeling of being part of a team and having done something out of the ordinary.

This sums Andy up, modest as ever. But as Trucker, an old army friend, pointed out, 'Andy is the type of person that wins Britain its wars': self-effacing, diligent, reliable and resilient. He had done the Royal Navy proud as part of our team and I am so pleased to have made a friend for life.

Some weeks after our return, out of the blue, Andy phoned me. He was on a run ashore in Scotland. He had been on board HMS *Newcastle*, the 425-foot destroyer he is stationed with, off the Scottish coast, and it had been blowing a gale. He had gone up to the bridge and stood transfixed.

'It was almost identical conditions to that storm we were in off Iceland,' he told me. 'Force Eights, howling winds and wild white horses everywhere.'

All he could see from the bridge was the foaming sea pouring over the decks of the ship, tonnes upon tonnes of white water. As he stared, he said, it was only then that he started to realize just what we had lived through.

'Maybe at the time your mind shuts out those feelings,' he said 'But there, on the bridge, all I could think was, to be out on that sea in a small RIB, you'd have to be suicidal.'

Nige reflects:

I suppose, more than anything, an experience like this expedition gives you a real sense of perspective. For me, I had never before felt my life was in danger, and certainly not for such a long period of time. I remember thinking, well, after dealing with that, how can a problem at work ever feel really serious, how can I ever be really worried by a deadline or an angry client?

Then that feeling wears off, and you soon get sucked back into a normal way of life again.

With hindsight, if I had known what it was going to be like, I'm not sure I would have joined the expedition, and I really don't want to put myself in such dangerous situations again.

All that said, it was a fantastic experience. I discovered how resilient I could be and, even if I never get any feeling back in my toes, because of the frostnip, I will always be grateful for that self-belief I have gained: that I can achieve something extraordinary.

Mick reflects:

When I returned home from Everest in 1998, I told people I had experienced a wider range of human emotions in three months on the mountain than in the twenty-three years of my life before that. My first response to this expedition is that I have similar feelings about those weeks on the ocean. It was unbelievably intense.

Whether I was feeling fear or friendship, it was a privilege to be involved and to be part of the team. We were a small, tight-knit group of men fighting through adversity to achieve a goal. When you are together like that, more than 300 miles from land, battling fierce seas and you're terrified for your life, that is when you start to understand the real value of life. You begin to know what it feels like to be truly alive.

I would do it all again tomorrow, but don't tell Mary or my

mother that. I think when you experience something like this, you learn to value life. It wakes you up a bit, and it reminds you that life can be amazing.

Each of us has a choice: you can either get out there and do something, or you can just sit on your arse and moan about work. I suppose we got out there, and it was brilliant. I wouldn't have missed it for the world.

Towards the end of the dinner at Kinloch, Mick stood up and said he wanted to tell me something. The room fell quiet, and I suddenly began to feel a bit embarrassed in front of everyone.

Mick looked at me, much more seriously now, and paused. He continued: 'I guess being a leader is all about coming through at the really key moments, and that moment in the middle of the night, in the middle of that storm, was when we really needed you, and you came through for us. On behalf of all your crew, I just want to say thank you for bringing us home safely.'

He reached over and shook my hand.

It was probably the nicest thing anyone has ever said to me.

14. HOME THOUGHTS

Good character is not given – we have to build it by thought, choice, courage and determination.

Mahatma Gandhi

The following morning, we waded out to the *Arnold and Son Explorer* and cruised along the coast to John O'Groats. Alex Rayner had all the press in place, and we approached the harbour waving the white ensign that the navy had lent us for this very moment. We all raised our arms – it was from relief more than triumph.

After an hour or so of interviews, we unpacked the RIB for the last time and took a few photos for ourselves. We then watched our pride and joy being dragged unceremoniously from the water by an old tractor, ready to be lifted on to the lorry that would carry her south. None of us knew what to think, and I, for one, suddenly felt a bit lost.

The atmosphere was lightened by an old lady who came up to Charlie as we were finishing the last few interviews, and looked him up and down very carefully.

'You're mad for sure, but how lucky you have been to have had such perfect weather for your crossing.' She smiled sweetly. Britain had been basking in a heatwave; she wasn't to know that for us, it had been the coldest time of our lives.

Charlie smiled back, shook her hand and signed her John O'Groats certificate graciously. We returned to Sam's house by road and prepared to catch the flight the following morning, from Inverness to Gatwick airport, where my wife and son would be waiting.

As I came through the arrivals lounge at Gatwick, I spotted them at once, Jesse held high on Shara's hip. His eyes were wide open, obsessed with seeing everything going on around him. Airports are serious fun, I saw him thinking. Shara's kiss told me I was truly home.

One morning, a few weeks later, I woke early and turned to look at Jesse asleep on the pillow beside me. He had woken early too and Shara had brought him through for a cuddle.

As I looked at his angelic, sleeping face, I realized it had been this little person, so innocent and powerless, who had sustained me through those stormy nights when I faced the very real prospect of never seeing him again, of not getting back to be his dad.

I thought how strange it was that during those crises he had wielded such power over me, yet he had no idea of what we went through, what had happened, no idea of the strength he helped me find.

Then I looked over at Shara, asleep as well. Together, side by side: my son and my wife. And right then I understood just how much they mean to me. They mean the world.

Sometimes I look back on all this and reckon I had to go a long way just to understand what I have at home.

Within five minutes of having stepped foot on dry land at John O'Groats, I got asked the inevitable question for the first time. I wasn't ready for it, and part of me couldn't believe someone had just asked it.

'So ... what's next, Bear?' the journalist inquired.

I was still in my dry-suit. I stared at him. I could hardly answer him. I hadn't even seen my family yet.

'Well, be sure to let us know,' he continued.

But the truth is, I'm not sure I want to put myself in that sort of danger again, not in that terrifying position where I stand no better than an even chance of coming home. I'm not sure I'm brave enough any longer.

If I really look inside me, I still find this fire burning, but it burns for my family. I want to be with them, to protect them and to mess about with them. I want to be a good husband, and I want to be as good a father for Jesse as my dad was for me. I want to teach him to sail and to climb. I want to be there. I don't want to disappear on some great expedition and not come home. A dead hero is worth nothing to a young boy.

And yet, isn't that what I do? Live on the edge? Try to be bold?

Maybe. But I also want to stay alive.

That's all.

The reality of the first few days, in fact weeks, after our return, was that so many people needed my time as well – from press to sponsors, to the navy, to the boat-builders. It seemed unending. I just craved peace and time – already.

Inevitably, a frenetic schedule developed. I had more

speaking engagements than ever before and within a week of our return we had done *Blue Peter, Good Morning,* BBC News, the Southampton Boat Show, CBBC and *London Tonight.* It was surreal.

We received so many kind letters from different people. They were all relieved to hear we had survived the crossing intact. One of the most lovely letters was from my great-uncle Edward, who, I think, captured the feelings of many of those who had followed our progress.

'Many congratulations on your achievement, to all five of you,' he wrote.

> Don't think that it has not caused your families and friends unbearable anxiety, particularly when your communication systems failed . . . The sea can be so menacing, please don't repeat anything so terrible again, if only to save your family from having sympathetic heart attacks. Which aged as old as I am is never a good thing.

Funny still, at ninety-three: fantastic.

Vice-Admiral Mark Stanhope, Deputy Commander-in-Chief Fleet, also took the trouble to write on behalf of the navy:

> With the successful conclusion of your epic voyage,
> I would like to offer you, on behalf of both myself and
> the First Sea Lord, my heartiest congratulations on your
> achievement. Crossing the Atlantic at any time can be a
> hairy experience and to have achieved it in a little RIB
> across the Arctic is a huge feat indeed. I for one was

closely monitoring your progress day by day, and we were all fully aware that you had some pretty appalling weather on some of the legs. But you did it. Well done you all, on getting home.

During one of our first free moments back in London, I grabbed time for a quick game of squash with my friend Ted Heywood. It was so good to be back and see Danny and Nicky and all my mates at the gym again. Ted began telling me with great relish how, completely by coincidence, his mother had been on a cruise ship, the *Pearl*, sailing around Iceland at the same time as us, in the same storm.

'Anyway,' Ted went on, 'she said they were caught in this huge squall. Well, at one point a wave hit the liner side-on, broaching the boat and dumping tonnes of icy water across the decks. Ornaments and cutlery slid across the tables and the captain made the decision to turn back. He decided conditions were so bad they could not continue.'

Danny shook his head at me, smiling. 'You daft bugger,' he said.

'And Bear,' Ted continued, 'those sorts of cruise ships don't just turn around in bad weather, especially when they have several hundred paying passengers on board.' The story put into stark perspective the conditions we had survived that night. I proceeded to lose the game of squash.

Other little things began to come out that confirmed just how lucky we had been to complete the expedition. After a series of public appearances, the boat was sent for an over-haul at MIT, the company that had supplied the jet drive and gear-box. The engineers there reported back that a belt in the engine had been incorrectly aligned and had become so worn that, in their estimation, it would not have lasted another twenty minutes at sea. They had never seen a belt that was so worn and yet, somehow, was still doing its job.

'That's OK,' I replied. 'We had two spares in the engine bay.'

'Yeah, we saw those too,' the engineer said. 'You had been supplied with spares that were the wrong size.'

Someone had been watching over us.

But there was more.

Subsequently, the RIB was based in the Solent, and one late afternoon, at the end of a sponsors' day out on the boat, we got a bit of rope caught in the jet intake. We had to be towed unceremoniously back into harbour, where we freed the rope and left the boat for the night, ready, we thought, for our next corporate day on her.

The phone rang at dawn next day. It was the boatman at Bembridge Sailing Club where she was moored. He was in a state. Water was pouring into the RIB. The jet housing was leaking. The aft tubes were under water, the engine had been flooded and the gear-box and electrics were being ruined. There was panic. We managed to recover her, but it took a month to repair her and a bill on our loyal Navigators and General Insurance tab of nearly £25,000.

If we had caught that bit of rope in the jet intake while arriving among one of the many small fishing communities that we visited – and it would have been the easiest thing in the world to do, especially since we so often arrived in the dark – the expedition would have been over.

We had been very fortunate; it seemed that God's Grace had followed us all the way home.

We had planned a party at St Katharine Docks in the City of London a week after our arrival back in the UK. This was partly to celebrate our safe return but mainly to thank our sponsors and formally to present a cheque to the Prince's Trust.

It was the most lovely of days. The sun shone, the five of us were wearing our expedition fleeces, and we were surrounded by all the people who had made the expedition possible: from our closest friends and families to Captain Pennefather; from our base team to all the lead sponsors – including Mattel Toys and the Computer Sciences Corporation.

As we neared the end of the day, Eric and Jean-Marie from Arnold and Son caught us by surprise when they presented us with an original letter, written by a famous old French explorer on Royal Geographical Society-headed paper. The letter was from one of the earliest polar challenges around the start of the last century. It was a lovely touch.

Will Young had agreed to accept the cheque on behalf of the Prince's Trust. As a fellow ambassador of the Trust, he had offered to come and support us. He was fantastic with everyone, including all the kids, and even tolerated two of my elderly relatives running up the walkway with their dicky legs and hips in an effort to get his autograph. I must admit

I was cringing a little at that point. But above all, he was just fun to have around.

'You must be so relieved,' Will said to me. He was right, but it seemed as if people had been saying exactly those words right from the start, and it had never been true before.

'You must be so relieved to have a sponsor' . . . 'You must be so relieved that the boat has arrived in Nova Scotia' . . . 'You must be so relieved that you had enough fuel to reach Greenland.'

And over and over again, I would smile and say, 'Well, sort of.'

The truth was, I never really felt relieved until after that final party at St Katharine Docks. Somehow I could never let it all go before then. There always seemed to be something else. But there wasn't now. At last.

That day in London, the sun had shone on us all afternoon but, just as the last guests left, it started to drizzle. Shara told me I was the 'jammiest man around'.

It was the perfect ending.

The five of us soon said our goodbyes and went our separate ways, back to our normal lives.

Now, as I reflect, my enduring image of the entire expedition is of five men who came together and made one fantastic team. Working as one, we had beaten the odds and survived.

Our strength was that we made decisions on instinct, pursued them with heart and soul and looked after one another when this was needed. We were a peculiar mix: a naval officer, a surveyor, an Internet businessman, a cameraman. They were just ordinary guys, but when it mattered, they came up with an extraordinary bravery and spirit.

Above everything, we were good friends.

Yes, I am proud of what we achieved, but I am much more proud of how we did it. The little things, like hearing Charlie tell his dad he couldn't believe there had not been any kind of cross word between us; listening to Mick thank me over dinner at Kinloch; the feeling of being hugged by Andy and Nige on the headland at John O'Groats. Those are the moments that really last.

Andy went straight back to work with the navy after stealing two days away with Lorraine and switching off his mobile phone. As far as everyone at work was concerned, he was 'defrosting'. He has been on board HMS *Newcastle* almost continually ever since.

Nige returned to Lunson Mitchenall, only to discover that on his first day back at work he was asked to attend a corporate boating day on the Solent – as if he had not had enough of the water for a while.

True to form, Mick changed from his expedition gear into his business suit and leaped straight back into the zone of building the Tiscali empire. But the Atlantic had taken its toll. Three weeks later, he phoned to say he was still feeling drained and exhausted. I was relieved to hear that someone else was also wiped out.

Charlie went back to Manchester and resumed his life as

a television cameraman. Part of this work meant we were still together, and he was the cameraman on an adventure series in the Brecon Beacons we were doing for Channel 4. Lying in a soaking ditch with me one night, up a mountain in Wales in sub-zero winter conditions, Charlie muttered that life had definitely got colder since we met. I apologized, laughing.

As for the sixth member of our team, our faithful boat, we finished the corporate days on her and said our farewells. We are currently in the process of trying to find a sponsor for her that will enable us to donate the boat to the sea-based charity the Meridian Trust. This trust offers disadvantaged kids the chance to experience the magic of the sea. I hope we manage to pull this off and allow these young people to benefit from this extraordinary craft. She was our life in those storms and never failed once. I hope others will grow to love her as we did.

For me, the experience of leadership had been much more demanding than I had ever imagined.

The bad part of me had hoped it would mean I would get more sleep, not less. I always assumed there would have to be some privileges for the leader of the expedition.

In practice, though, to lead properly, you end up being the last one to go to bed at night, and the first one to wake in the morning. There were times when Andy had to wake at 5 a.m. to change the oil filters, so I would aim to get up with him to have a cup of tea together first. Then, in the afternoon, while Andy might be grabbing an hour of sleep, I would be with Mick checking the weather forecasts on the Internet.

As somebody who in previous expeditions had always taken great pleasure in oversleeping, the responsibility of leadership was something that required me to give my all. That is a good thing: the result was worth it. Every time.

But what *would* be next? This time the question wasn't coming from some journalist; it was coming from within me.

Sometimes I sense that people live their own dreams through explorers. It is a form of escape from life, something safe upon which to quench their thirst for danger. But I am not sure I want to be the sacrifice for these people's urges any longer.

When asked 'What next?', the easy answer is to say K2, or the South Pole. It all rolls off the tongue so easily. But in many ways it is a coward's answer.

Explorers, climbers and sailors are meant to be brave. But so often we aren't brave enough to be honest.

Honest enough to say, 'I am feeling a bit frightened of those things at the moment.'

Honest enough to say, 'You've caught me at a very vulnerable time, and I am not sure I have an answer right now.'

I hope I am brave enough to say all this.

But I know for certain that life is so much more than always having to top something or better the last achievement.

That's not the way I want to lead my life.

We all so often live in the shadow of people's expectations. But as soon as we do that, we lose our power. The magic dies. I don't want that. I hope to keep living as I have always lived – by heart.

I hope always to be among the elements, to be in beautiful, isolated places, far from the big cities, places where life is simple and pure, places where I can feel God's quiet presence around me.

I want to keep connecting with people, whether in a small boat or on a mountain, in an audience or on the TV; even in a book. It is all about giving humanity. It's about being brutally straight with yourself, even to your own detriment. That is sometimes so hard to do.

I want people to know I am normal, with just as many doubts and weaknesses and struggles as anyone else, but if we can just hang on, we can come through – and maybe even find ourselves a little stronger.

For us, though, the truth is we got lucky on Everest, and we got lucky on the frozen North Atlantic; and you don't have to be a mathematician to realize that you can't keep playing those sorts of odds and always win.

I only have to think of my late friend, Ginette Harrison, whom I first met while climbing in Nepal. We were together on the so-called unclimbable mountain, Ama Dablam, in the Himalayas. It was the year before our attempt on Everest. Ginette was a kind, strong, beautiful woman, and probably the best female climber of her age. She was intelligent and cautious and, in my eyes, as a climber, she was nothing less than invincible.

However, two years later, back in the Himalayas she was attempting to climb another great peak. Just one more. She was struck by an avalanche and killed. Just like that. Only a month earlier we had been having lunch together in London.

The avalanche wasn't her fault. She had done nothing wrong. Humans are strong, but nature is stronger. And if you play the odds long enough, it is true: you cannot always win.

But I am no longer prepared to die on some distant mountain or senseless sea. And if I have learned anything from these wild forces of nature, it is a quiet determination to stay alive.

Several months later, the Royal Geographical Society hosted the crew of the Arnold and Son Transatlantic Arctic Expedition to give a presentation on our experiences. The five of us gathered at the awe-inspiring, historic venue, on the south side of London's Hyde Park, and we told our story.

At the end of the evening, I stood up to conclude. I noticed the side door open, and some light fill the room. It was Shara re-emerging into the hall, carrying Jesse in her arms. He was meant to be in bed – it was 8.30 p.m., but she had arranged for him to be here.

On impulse, I stepped down from the stage and took him in my arms. We all then stood onstage together: the team and myself, with Jesse wrapped up in a little blanket. As he peeked out from under his little hat at the sea of faces, I had never felt so proud.

Not long afterwards, Jesse was christened on our barge, just as I had always hoped he would be.

Nicky, the priest, stood on the upper deck, and his robes billowed in the autumn breeze that whistles down the Thames.

He reached for the little bottle of snow water that I had brought back from the summit of Everest some five years ago and had kept for this very occasion. He dabbed it on Jesse's tiny forehead. And right there, he christened our lovely son.

Right from the start, this had been the plan.

And the plan had worked. By Grace.

I hope Jesse's grandfather, my late dad, felt proud.

If I go up to the Heavens, you are there;
if I go down to the place of the dead, you are there also.
If I ride the morning wind to the ends of the ocean,
even there your hand will guide,
your strength will support me...
I can never be lost to your Spirit.

Psalm 139:5–10

Don't be afraid to go on the odd wild goose chase,
that's what wild geese are for!

Anon.

GLOSSARY

EPIRB frequencies – Emergency Position Indicating Radio
Beacon. A globally detectable, emergency broadcast signal
sent via satellite and transmitted on the 406MHz frequency

GPS – Global Positioning System. Signals from 24 satellites
provide precise geodetic positioning and navigation

prop – propeller

payloads – weight

helming – steering

lifelines – ropes running the length of a boat on to which a
sailor clips his safety harness

stern – back of a boat

bow – front end of a boat

prow – front of a boat

foredeck – front deck of a boat

hull – the body or bottom of a boat

jet housing – the casing for the internal propeller

lee – sheltered side

fenders – buffers slung over the sides of the boat to protect it
from damage

parachute sea anchor – an anchor for use in deep water.
The 'parachute', which is made of fabric, fills with water
and holds the boat in place

Gortex – air-permeable waterproof material

GLOSSARY

chandlery – a store selling boating supplies

jet drive – a form of propulsion for a boat

beam seas – where the waves arrive side-on to the boat

head sea – where the waves arrive head-on to the boat

ACKNOWLEDGEMENTS

Sponsors of www.arctic2003.com

Title Sponsor

Arnold and Son Watches, British Masters,
Switzerland and London

Lead Sponsors

Royal Navy   Daily Telegraph   Shell
BT Exact and NVP Brightstar   Lafarge Aggregates   CSC
Lunson Mitchenall   London Speaker Bureau
MIT Group – Twin Disc   Davis Langdon UK   Vitol
Simrad   Finnings CAT   Sage   Mattel – Hot Wheels
General Motors (Canada)

With special thanks to

HRH The Prince of Wales   British Airways plc
The Royal Geographical Society, London
The Canadian Navy   The Danish Navy
London and Southampton Boat Shows   Schroders
E Squadron, 21st Special Air Service   Musto Clothing
White Stuff Clothing   Navigators and General Insurance

ACKNOWLEDGEMENTS

Gecko Headgear   Professor Robert Swan

Ocean Dynamics RIBs   Mustang Marine

Gunwharf Quay, Portsmouth   Food Ferry – supplies

Deliverance – supplies   Bembridge Sailing Club

Echomax – radar reflectors   C-Map – charts   MarineTrack

Sartech – survival equipment   Barnstead Int. Electro-thermal

Soltron – fuel additive   Dampire – kit-drying systems

Nova Scotia Sailing School   Rightons Aluminium

Seastart – recovery   Pan Macmillan

Peter Fraser and Dunlop Literary Agents

George and Carol McFadden   Bruce Cameron

Morris and Jill Marshment   Cranham Builders

The Crosthwaite family   The Laing family

The Thompson family   The Liever family

The Proctor family   The Vyner-Brooks family

Ed Griffiths and family   The McGregor family   Hy Money

Ludgrove School   Canons Gym   Dronsfield Technologies

www.octavianart.com   Stargate3 Satellite Communications

Iridium satellite technology   Carabina Logistics

FPT Industries – fuel systems   Sigma Displays

Wallenius Wilhelmsen Lines UK – boat transport

Premier Promotions   Mumm Champagne

Cunningham Management   Liaison Media – PR

Whitbread Foundation   Cosalt – life rafts

Ocean Safety supplies   Col Henry Hughe-Smith

NSA Int. Juice Plus +   Alpine Club

Royal Navy Sailing Centre

SAS Regimental Association

The Charity

The Prince's Trust strives to help fourteen- to thirty-year-olds develop confidence, learn new skills, get into work and start businesses. Their message, 'Yes You Can', encourages young people to believe in themselves whatever obstacles they face.

Bear Grylls has been an ambassador for the Prince's Trust since 2003 and is also now Chief Scout and figurehead to 28 million Scouts worldwide, a post that encourages young people to learn adventure skills and enjoy the outdoors with good friends.

For further information on the Prince's Trust, see:
www.princes-trust.org.uk.

For further information on Bear Grylls, see:
www.beargrylls.com.